English/Korean Edition

The New Oxford Picture Dictionary

E. C. Parnwell

W9-BAE-746

Translated by Andrew-Inseok Kim

Illustrations by:
Ray Burns
Bob Giuliani
Laura Hartman
Pamela Johnson
Melodye Rosales
Raymond Skibinski
Joel Snyder

Oxford University Press

Oxford University Press

198 Madison Avenue
New York, NY 10016 USA

Great Clarendon Street
Oxford OX2 6DP England

OXFORD is a trademark of Oxford University Press.

ISBN 0-19-434360-X

Associate Editor: Mary Lynne Nielsen
Assistant Editor: Mary Sutherland
Art Director: Lynn Luchetti
Production Co-ordinator: Claire Nicholl
The publishers would like to thank the following agents for their co-operation:
Carol Bancroft and Friends, representing Bob Giuliani,
Laura Hartman, and Melodye Rosales.

Publishers Graphics Inc., representing Ray Burns,
Pamela Johnson, and Joel Snyder.

Cover illustration by Laura Hartman.

Printing (last digit): 9

Printed in Hong Kong

The New Oxford Picture Dictionary contextually illustrates over 2,400 words. The book is a unique language learning tool for students of English. It provides students with a glance at American lifestyle, as well as a compendium of useful vocabulary.

The *Dictionary* is organized thematically, beginning with topics that are most useful for the "survival" needs of students in an English-speaking country. However, pages may be used at random, depending on the students' particular needs. The book need not be taught in order.

The New Oxford Picture Dictionary contextualizes vocabulary whenever possible. Verbs have been included on separate pages, but within a topic area where they are most likely to occur. However, this does not imply that these verbs only appear within these contexts.

Articles are shown only with irregular nouns. Regional variations of the primary translation are listed following a slash (/). A complete index with pronunciation guide in English is in the Appendix.

For further ideas on using *The New Oxford Picture Dictionary*, see the *Listening and Speaking Activity Book,* the *Teacher's Guide,* and the two workbooks: *Beginner's* and *Intermediate* levels. Also available in the program are a complete set of *Cassettes,* offering a reading of all the words in the *Dictionary; Vocabulary Playing Cards,* featuring 40 words and the corresponding prictures on 80 cards, with ideas for many games; sets of *Wall Charts,* available in one complete package, or in three smaller packages; and *Overhead Transparencies,* featuring color transparencies of all the *Dictionary* pages (all of these items are available in English only). The *NOPD CD-ROM* offers the *Dictionary* in an interactive multimedia format and includes exercises and activities.

옥스포드 새 그림 사전 (The New Oxford Picture Dictionary)은 2,400개의 단어를 그림과 함께 수록합니다. 이 책은 영어를 배우는 학생들에게 매우 유익한 학습 자료가 됩니다. 학생들에게 미국 생활상을 한눈에 보여 줄 뿐만 아니라, 생활에 필요한 단어를 수록한 참고서로서도 가치가 있습니다.

이 사전은 영어가 모국어로 쓰이는 국가에서 사는 학생들이 기본 의사 소통을 하는데 꼭 필요한 것부터 시작하여, 주제별로 구성되어 있습니다. 그러나, 학생들의 특별한 필요에 따라 어느 면에서든지 학습을 시작할 수 있기때문에, 순서대로 가르치실 필요가 없습니다.

옥스포드 새 그림 사전은 단어를 가능한 한 상황을 들어 설명하였습니다. 동사는 유형별로 모아 별도의 면에 수록되어 있으나, 그렇다고 하여 동사가 꼭 이러한 상황에서만 쓰인다는 것을 의미하지는 않습니다.

영어 발음 해설을 담은 완전한 색인이 부록편에 있으며, 한국어 색인도 포함되어 있습니다.

이 사전의 이용도에 대하여 보다 더 알고자 하시는 분은 교사 지침서와 초급. 중급 학습서를 참고로 하실 수 있습니다. 또한 이 프로그램의 일부로, 사전에 수록된 전 단어의 발음을 녹음한 카셋트, 여러 가지 게임을 위한 아이디어로서 40개의 단어와 그에 해당되는 카드 80장과 벽도표가 완전하게 구비되어 있습니다. 이것을 한꺼번에 또는 3등분하여 구입하실 수 있습니다.

ii Contents

목 차

People and Relationships 사람과 그 관계   *Page* 2
The Family 가족   3
The Human Body 인체 구조   4–5
Vegetables 야채류   6–7
Fruits 과일류   8–9
Meat, Poultry, and Seafood 고기, 가금 및 해물류   10–11
Containers, Quantities, and Money 용기, 분량 및 화폐   12–13
The Supermarket 수퍼마켓   14–15
Family Restaurant and Cocktail Lounge 가족용 식당과 칵테일 라운지   16
Restaurant Verbs 식당에서 쓰이는 동사   17
Common Prepared Foods 흔히 요리되어 있는 음식   18
Outdoor Clothes 야외복   19
Everyday Clothes 평상복   20–21
Underwear and Sleepwear 속옷 및 잠옷   22
Jewelry and Cosmetics 보석류 및 화장품   23
Describing Clothes 의복을 설명하는데 쓰이는 말   24
Describing the Weather 날씨를 설명하는데 쓰이는 말   25
Seasonal Verbs 계절에 관한 동사   26
Houses 주택   27
The Living Room 거실   28
The Dining Room 식당방   29
The Kitchen 부엌   30
Kitchen Verbs 부엌에서 요리할 때 쓰이는 동사   31
The Bedroom 침실   32
The Baby's Room 갓난 아기방   33
The Bathroom 화장실   34
The Utility Room 다용도실   35
A Workshop 작업장   36–37
Housework and Repair Verbs 집안일과 수선하는데 쓰이는 동사   38
Medical and Dental Care 의과 및 치과 치료   39
Ailments and Injuries 가벼운 질병 및 상처   40
Treatments and Remedies 치료 및 구제법   41
Firefighting and Rescue 진화 작업 및 구조   42
Crime and Punishment 범죄 및 처벌   43
The City 도시   44–45
The U.S. Postal System 미국 우편국 제도   46
The Public Library 공공 도서관   47
The Armed Forces 군대 : 육·해·공군   48
Trucks 트럭   49
Cars 자동차   50–51
Bikes 자전거   52
Highway Travel 고속도로 여행   53
Public Transportation 공공 운송기관   54–55
Air Travel 항공 여행   56
Aircraft 항공기   57
In Port 항구   58
Pleasure Boating 유흥 뱃놀이   59
Plants and Trees 식물 및 나무   60–61
Simple Animals 간단한 동물   62
Insects 곤충   63
Birds 새   64
Fish and Reptiles 물고기 및 파충류   65
Mammals I 포유동물 I   66–67
Mammals II 포유동물 II   68–69
Map of the World 세계지도   70–71
The United States of America 미합중국의 주명칭   72–73
The Universe 우주   74
The Space Program 우주 프로그램   75

Contents iii
목 차

A Classroom 교실   *Page*   76
School Verbs 학교에서 쓰이는 동사   77
A Science Lab 과학 실험실   78
Math 수학   79
Energy 에너지   80
Farming and Ranching 농업 및 목축업   81
Construction 건축공사   82
An Office 사무실   83
Occupations I: Main Street USA 직업 I : 미국의 주된 업종   84
Occupations II 직업 II   85
Occupations III 직업 III   86
Neighborhood Parks 동네 공원   87
Outdoor Activities 야영 활동   88–89
At the Beach 해변 가에서   90–91
Team Sports 단체 운동 경기   92
Ballfields 구기 시합장   93
Individual Sports 개인 스포츠   94
Fields and Courses 필드 및 코스 경기   95
Sports Verbs 운동에 관한 동사   96–97
Musical Instruments 악기   98
Music, Dance, and Theater 음악, 댄스 및 극장   99
Electronics and Photography 전자제품 및 사진술   100
Handicrafts 수세공   101
Prepositions of Description 위치에 관한 전치사   102
Prepositions of Motion 이동에 관한 전치사   103
Appendix 부록   104
Index 색인   105

사람과 그 관계

여자	**1.** woman		어린이	**7.** children
남자	**2.** man		소년	**8.** boy
남편	**3.** husband		소녀	**9.** girl
아내	**4.** wife		조부모	**10.** grandparents
아기	**5.** baby		손녀	**11.** granddaughter
부모	**6.** parents		손자	**12.** grandson

Virginia (Taylor) Bates (1)

Joseph Bates (2)

Ellen (Dalton) Bates

Peter Bates (3)

Elizabeth (Bates) Jones (4)

Tom Jones (5)

Helen Jones (6)

Joan Bates (7)

Betty (Collins) Jones (8)

Jack Jones (9)

Jane (Jones) Carter (10)

Tom Carter (11)

Mary (Jones) Smith

Bob Smith (12)

Jimmy Lee Jones (13)

Peg Carter (14)

Sally Ann Smith (15)

Tim Smith (16)

메리 스미스씨의 가족	**Mary Smith's Family**		
할머니	**1.** grandmother	형제	**9.** brother
할아버지	**2.** grandfather	자매	**10.** sister
삼촌	**3.** uncle	매형, 매제	**11.** brother-in-law
어머니	**4.** mother	남편	**12.** husband
아버지	**5.** father	조카	**13.** nephew
아주머니	**6.** aunt	조카딸(질녀)	**14.** niece
사촌	**7.** cousin	딸	**15.** daughter
형수, 올케	**8.** sister-in-law	아들	**16.** son

인체 구조

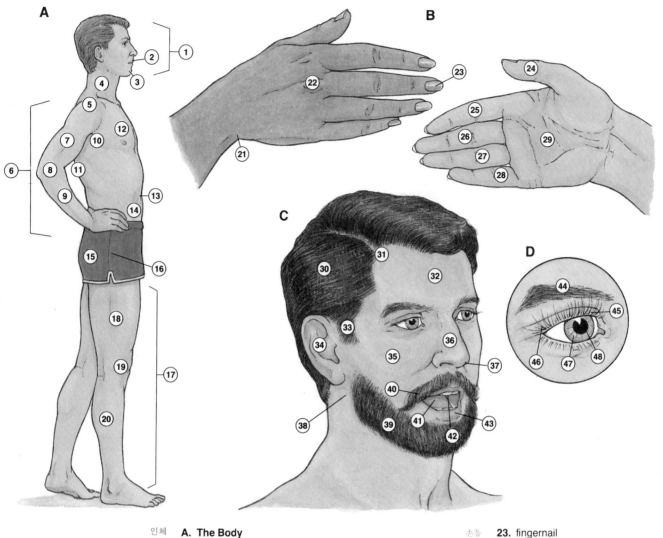

인체	**A. The Body**		손톱	**23.** fingernail
얼굴	**1.** face		엄지	**24.** thumb
입	**2.** mouth		집게 손가락	**25.** (index) finger
턱	**3.** chin		가운뎃 손가락	**26.** middle finger
목	**4.** neck		약 손가락	**27.** ring finger
어깨	**5.** shoulder		새끼 손가락	**28.** little finger
팔	**6.** arm		손바닥	**29.** palm
윗팔	**7.** upper arm			
팔꿈치	**8.** elbow		머리	**C. The Head**
팔뚝	**9.** forearm		머리카락	**30.** hair
겨드랑이	**10.** armpit		가르마	**31.** part
등	**11.** back		이마	**32.** forehead
가슴	**12.** chest		짧은 구렛나루(귀옆머리)	**33.** sideburn
허리	**13.** waist		귀	**34.** ear
배	**14.** abdomen		볼	**35.** cheek
엉덩이	**15.** buttocks		코	**36.** nose
골반	**16.** hip		콧구멍	**37.** nostril
다리	**17.** leg		턱	**38.** jaw
허벅지	**18.** thigh		구렛나루	**39.** beard
무릎	**19.** knee		콧수염	**40.** mustache
장딴지	**20.** calf		혀	**41.** tongue
			이빨	**42.** tooth
손	**B. The Hand**		입술	**43.** lip
팔목	**21.** wrist			
손등	**22.** knuckle			

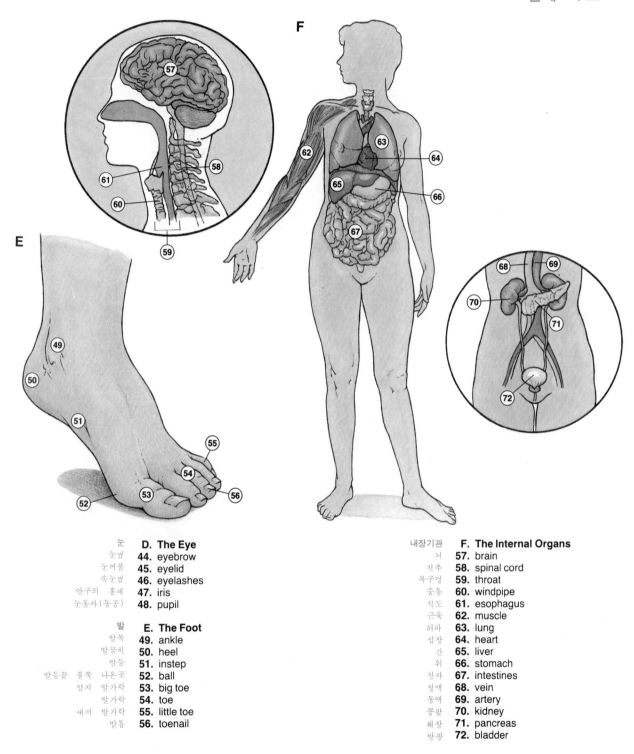

	D. The Eye
눈	
눈썹	**44.** eyebrow
눈꺼풀	**45.** eyelid
속눈썹	**46.** eyelashes
안구의 홍채	**47.** iris
눈동자(동공)	**48.** pupil

	E. The Foot
발	
발목	**49.** ankle
발꿈치	**50.** heel
발등	**51.** instep
발등끝 불쑥 나온곳	**52.** ball
엄지 발가락	**53.** big toe
발가락	**54.** toe
새끼 발가락	**55.** little toe
발톱	**56.** toenail

	F. The Internal Organs
내장기관	
뇌	**57.** brain
척추	**58.** spinal cord
목구멍	**59.** throat
숨통	**60.** windpipe
식도	**61.** esophagus
근육	**62.** muscle
허파	**63.** lung
심장	**64.** heart
간	**65.** liver
위	**66.** stomach
창자	**67.** intestines
정맥	**68.** vein
동맥	**69.** artery
콩팥	**70.** kidney
췌장	**71.** pancreas
방광	**72.** bladder

컬리플라워	**1.** (head of) cauliflower	아티초크	**11.** artichoke
보로컬리	**2.** broccoli	옥수수	**12.** (ear of) corn
배추	**3.** cabbage	옥수수속	**a.** cob
애기양배추	**4.** brussels sprouts	강낭콩	**13.** kidney bean(s)
미나리	**5.** watercress	팥	**14.** black bean(s)
상치	**6.** lettuce	깍지 강낭콩	**15.** string bean(s)
꽃상치	**7.** escarole	리마콩	**16.** lima bean(s)
시금치	**8.** spinach	완두콩	**17.** pea(s)
향초	**9.** herb(s)	완두콩 꼬투리	**a.** pod
셀러리	**10.** celery	아스파라거스	**18.** asparagus

토마토	**19.** tomato(es)		긴호박	**27.** zucchini
오이	**20.** cucumber(s)		도토리호박	**28.** acorn squash
가지	**21.** eggplant		빨간 무우	**29.** radish(es)
고추	**22.** pepper(s)		버섯	**30.** mushroom(s)
감자	**23.** potato(es)		양파	**31.** onion(s)
고구마	**24.** yam		당근	**32.** carrot(s)
마늘	**25.** garlic		근대	**33.** beet(s)
마늘쪽	**a.** clove		순무뿌리	**34.** turnip
호박	**26.** pumpkin			

포도	**1.** (a bunch of) grapes
사과	**2.** apple
꼭지	**a.** stem
씨	**b.** core
코코넛	**3.** coconut
파인애플	**4.** pineapple
망고	**5.** mango
파파야	**6.** papaya
신과일류	**Citrus Fruits**
그레이프프루트	**7.** grapefruit
귤	**8.** orange
귤 조각	**a.** section
귤 껍질	**b.** rind
씨	**c.** seed

레몬	**9.** lemon
라임	**10.** lime
딸기류	**Berries**
꽈리	**11.** gooseberries
검은 딸기	**12.** blackberries
넝쿨월귤	**13.** cranberries
푸른 딸기	**14.** blueberries
딸기	**15.** strawberry
나무딸기	**16.** raspberries
승도복숭아	**17.** nectarine
배	**18.** pear

앵두	**19.** cherries
바나나	**20.** (a bunch of) bananas
껍질	**a.** peel
마른과일류	**Dried Fruits**
무화과	**21.** fig
대추	**22.** prune
말린자두	**23.** date
건포도	**24.** raisin(s)
살구	**25.** apricot
수박	**26.** watermelon

견과류	**Nuts**
캐슈	**27.** cashew(s)
땅콩	**28.** peanut(s)
호도	**29.** walnut(s)
개암	**30.** hazelnut(s)
아몬드	**31.** almond(s)
밤	**32.** chestnut(s)
아보카도	**33.** avocado
자두	**34.** plum
감로멜론	**35.** honeydew melon
캔탈로프	**36.** cantaloupe
복숭아	**37.** peach
복숭아씨	**a.** pit
껍질	**b.** skin

고기, 가금 및 해물류

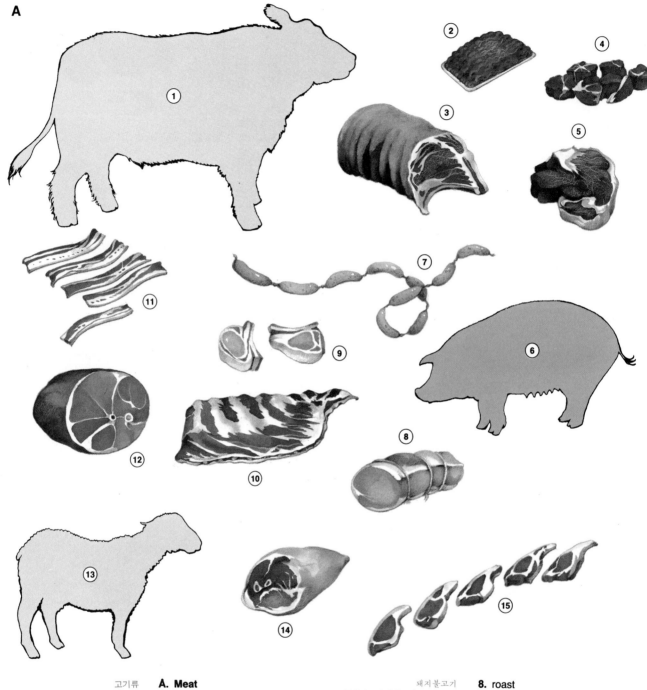

고기류	**A. Meat**	돼지불고기	**8.** roast
쇠고기	**1.** beef	두껍게 베어낸 돼지 고깃점	**9.** chops
간고기	**2.** ground beef	갈비	**10.** spare ribs
소불고기	**3.** roast	베이컨	**11.** bacon
졸임용 고기	**4.** stewing meat	햄	**12.** ham
스테이크	**5.** steak	양고기	**13.** lamb
돼지고기	**6.** pork	다리	**14.** leg
소세지	**7.** sausage	양고깃점	**15.** chops

가금류	B. Poultry	통생선	27. whole
통닭	16. whole (chicken)	생선포	28. filet
반쪽닭	17. split	스테이크용 생선 도막	29. steak
4등분 닭	18. quarter		
허벅지	19. thigh	조개류	D. Shellfish
다리	20. leg	바닷가재	30. lobster
가슴	21. breast	새우	31. shrimp
날개	22. wing	대합	32. clam(s)
칠면조	23. turkey	굴	33. oyster(s)
닭고기	24. chicken	홍합	34. mussel(s)
오리	25. duck	가리비	35. scallop(s)
		게	36. crab(s)
해물류	C. Seafood		
생선	26. fish		

용기, 분량 및 화폐

판지로 만든 상자	**1.** carton
그릇	**2.** container
병	**3.** bottle
포장	**4.** package
막대기 모양의 물건	**5.** stick
통	**6.** tub

빵 덩어리	**7.** loaf
봉지	**8.** bag
병	**9.** jar
깡통	**10.** can
두루마리	**11.** roll

상자	**12.**	box
6 개들이 한벌	**13.**	six-pack
펌프	**14.**	pump
튜브	**15.**	tube
한벌	**16.**	pack
한 봉지	**17.**	book
한개	**18.**	bar
찻잔	**19.**	cup
유리잔	**20.**	glass
(베어낸) 한조각	**21.**	slice
한조각	**22.**	piece

사발, 공기	**23.**	bowl
뿌리개 통	**24.**	spray can
화폐		**Money**
지폐	**25.**	dollar bills
동전	**26.**	coins
일전	**27.**	penny
오전	**28.**	nickel
십전	**29.**	dime
이십오전	**30.**	quarter

조제 식품점	**1.** deli counter	쇼핑 바구리	**8.** shopping basket
냉동 식품	**2.** frozen foods	야채	**9.** produce
냉동실	**3.** freezer	통로, 복도	**10.** aisle
우유제품	**4.** dairy products	구운 제품	**11.** baked goods
우유	**5.** milk	빵	**12.** bread
선반	**6.** shelf	통조림	**13.** canned goods
저울	**7.** scale	음료수	**14.** beverages

FISH MEAT POULTRY

EXPRESS LANE 10 ITEMS OR LESS

가정용품	**15.** household items		회계원	**22.** cashier
저장통	**16.** bin		이동용 벨트	**23.** conveyor belt
손님	**17.** customer		식료품	**24.** groceries
간식	**18.** snacks		봉지	**25.** bag
손 수레	**19.** shopping cart		계산대	**26.** checkout counter
영수증	**20.** receipt		수표	**27.** check
계산기	**21.** cash register			

가족용 식당과 칵테일 라운지

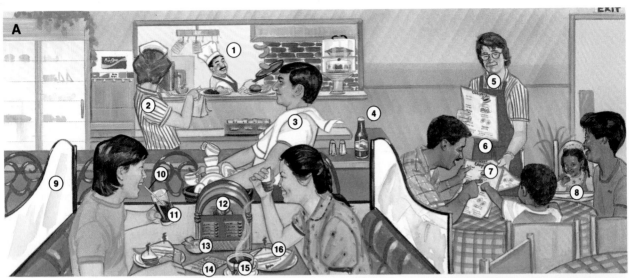

가족용 식당	**A. Family Restaurant**	칵테일 라운지	**B. Cocktail Lounge**
요리사	**1.** cook	마개 뽑이	**17.** corkscrew
여종업원	**2.** waitress	마개	**18.** cork
조수	**3.** busboy	포도주	**19.** wine
케첩	**4.** ketchup	꼭지	**20.** tap
남종업원	**5.** waiter	술집 지배인	**21.** bartender
앞치마	**6.** apron	술	**22.** liquor (bottle)
식단표	**7.** menu	맥주	**23.** beer
어린이용 의자	**8.** high chair	손님이 둘러 앉는 바	**24.** bar
칸막은 좌석	**9.** booth	손님용 높은 의자	**25.** bar stool
빨대	**10.** straw	담뱃대	**26.** pipe
청량음료	**11.** soft drink	받침접시	**27.** coaster
자동전축	**12.** jukebox	종이성냥	**28.** (book of) matches
설탕	**13.** sugar (packet)	재떨이	**29.** ashtray
계산서	**14.** check	라이터	**30.** lighter
차	**15.** tea	담배	**31.** cigarette
샌드위치	**16.** sandwich	여종업원	**32.** cocktail waitress
		쟁반	**33.** tray

먹다	**1.** eat	정리하다	**8.** set (the table)
마시다	**2.** drink	주다	**9.** give
접대하다	**3.** serve	가져가다	**10.** take
요리하다	**4.** cook	퍼 바르다	**11.** spread
주문하다	**5.** order	들다	**12.** hold
치우다	**6.** clear	불 붙이다	**13.** light
계산하다	**7.** pay	타다	**14.** burn

혼히 요리되어 있는 음식

겨자	**1.** mustard	롤빵	**19.** roll
핫도그	**2.** hot dog	군감자	**20.** baked potato
구워낸 콩	**3.** baked beans	스테이크	**21.** steak
감자깡	**4.** potato chips	과자	**22.** cookie
팬케이크	**5.** pancakes	아이스크림 선데이	**23.** sundae
물엿	**6.** syrup	고기와 양상치가 든 옥수수빵	**24.** taco
둥그런 빵	**7.** bun	달걀말이 튀김	**25.** egg roll
절인 오이지	**8.** pickle	딸기 케이크	**26.** strawberry shortcake
햄버거	**9.** hamburger	비스커트	**27.** biscuit
스파게티	**10.** spaghetti	감자튀김	**28.** french fries
고기완자	**11.** meatballs	튀긴닭	**29.** fried chicken
샐러드용 드레싱	**12.** salad dressing	피자	**30.** pizza
드레싱친 샐러드	**13.** tossed salad	젤리	**31.** jelly
소고기 졸임	**14.** beef stew	달걀후라이	**32.** (sunnyside-up) egg
고기붙은 돼지갈비	**15.** pork chops	베이컨	**33.** bacon
섞인 야채	**16.** mixed vegetables	구운빵	**34.** toast
으깬 감자	**17.** mashed potatoes	커피	**35.** coffee
버터	**18.** butter	아이스크림 콘	**36.** ice cream cone

장갑	**1.** gloves		보온 털실 양말	**14.** tights
모자	**2.** cap		스케이트 구두날	**15.** ice skates
면사쓰	**3.** flannel shirt		스키모자	**16.** ski cap
등짐용 가방	**4.** backpack		잠바	**17.** jacket
바람막이용 잠바	**5.** windbreaker		모자	**18.** hat
청바지	**6.** (blue) jeans		목도리	**19.** scarf
목스웨터	**7.** (crewneck) sweater		오바	**20.** overcoat
두건달린 모피옷	**8.** parka		반장화	**21.** boots
도보용 반장화	**9.** hiking boots		베레모	**22.** beret
귀마개	**10.** earmuffs		V자형 스웨터	**23.** (V-neck) sweater
벙어리 장갑	**11.** mittens		외투	**24.** coat
조끼	**12.** down vest		비장화	**25.** rain boots
자라목 스웨터	**13.** (turtleneck) sweater			

양복의 접은 옷깃	**1.** lapel
스포츠용 상의	**2.** blazer
단추	**3.** button
느슨한 바지	**4.** slacks
구두뒷굽	**5.** heel
구두밑창	**6.** sole
구두끈	**7.** shoelace
두껍고 헐거운 스웨터	**8.** sweatshirt
지갑	**9.** wallet
헐렁한 바지	**10.** sweatpants
운동화	**11.** sneakers
머리띠	**12.** sweatband
수영복 모양의 웃옷	**13.** tank top

반바지	**14.** shorts
긴소매	**15.** long sleeve
허리띠	**16.** belt
혁대	**17.** buckle
쇼핑가방	**18.** shopping bag
샌들	**19.** sandal
접어 젖힌 깃	**20.** collar
짧은소매	**21.** short sleeve
여성용 드레스	**22.** dress
핸드백	**23.** purse
우산	**24.** umbrella
굽이 높은 구두	**25.** (high) heels

앞을 단추로 채우는 스웨터	**26.** cardigan
고르덴 바지	**27.** (corduroy) pants
안전모	**28.** hard hat
T - 자형 샤쓰	**29.** T-shirt
작업 바지	**30.** overalls
도시락통	**31.** lunch box
작업화	**32.** (construction) boots
웃옷	**33.** jacket
블라우스	**34.** blouse
어깨에 메는 가방	**35.** (shoulder) bag
치마	**36.** skirt
서류 가방	**37.** briefcase

비옷	**38.** raincoat
조끼	**39.** vest
셋 갖춤 양복	**40.** three-piece suit
호주머니	**41.** pocket
간편화	**42.** loafer
모자	**43.** cap
안경	**44.** glasses
제복	**45.** uniform
와이 샤쓰	**46.** shirt
넥타이	**47.** tie
신문	**48.** newspaper
구두	**49.** shoe

속옷 및 잠옷

메리야스	**1.** undershirt		짧은팬티	**12.** briefs
반바지	**2.** boxer shorts		브라자	**13.** bra(ssiere)
팬티	**3.** underpants		가터밸트	**14.** garter belt
운동선수 밑받침	**4.** athletic supporter		거들	**15.** girdle
팬티호즈	**5.** pantyhose		무릎 양말	**16.** knee socks
스타킹	**6.** stockings		양말	**17.** socks
내의	**7.** long johns		슬리퍼	**18.** slippers
반속치마	**8.** half slip		남성용 잠옷	**19.** pajamas
캐미솔	**9.** camisole		목욕용 실내복	**20.** bathrobe
속치마	**10.** full slip		여성·아이들의 잠옷	**21.** nightgown
삼각팬티	**11.** (bikini) panties			

보석류	**A. Jewelry**	화장실용품 및 화장품류	**B. Toiletries and Makeup**
귀거리	1. earrings	면도기	20. razor
반지	2. ring(s)	면도후 바르는 로숀	21. after-shave lotion
약혼반지	3. engagement ring	면도용 크림	22. shaving cream
결혼반지	4. wedding ring	면도 칼	23. razor blades
줄보석	5. chain	손톱 줄	24. emery board
목걸이	6. necklace	메니큐어용 에나멜	25. nail polish
염주 목걸이	7. (strand of) beads	눈썹연필	26. eyebrow pencil
핀(브로치)	8. pin	향수	27. perfume
팔찌	9. bracelet	마스카라	28. mascara
시계	10. watch	입술연지	29. lipstick
시계줄	11. watchband	아이새도	30. eye shadow
소맷부리 단추	12. cuff links	손톱깎이	31. nail clippers
넥타이 핀	13. tie pin	분 바르개	32. blush
넥타이 클립	14. tie clip	아이라이너	33. eyeliner
클립 귀걸이	15. clip-on earring		
구멍 뚫림용 귀걸이	16. pierced earring		
걸쇠	17. clasp		
잠근쇠 촉	18. post		
잠근쇠 촉받이	19. back		

의복을 설명하는데 쓰이는 말

짧은	**1.** short		낮은	**12.** low
긴	**2.** long		새로운	**13.** new
꼭낀	**3.** tight		낡은	**14.** old
헐거운	**4.** loose		열린	**15.** open
지저분한	**5.** dirty		닫힌	**16.** closed
깨끗한	**6.** clean		줄무늬가 있는	**17.** striped
작은	**7.** small		바둑판 무늬가 있는	**18.** checked
큰	**8.** big		폴카 점이 있는	**19.** polka dot
엷은	**9.** light		빽빽이 짠	**20.** solid
짙은	**10.** dark		무늬를 날염한	**21.** print
높은	**11.** high		격자 무늬의	**22.** plaid

날씨를 설명하는데 쓰이는 말

비가 오는	**1.** rainy		쌀쌀한	**9.** cool
구름이 낀	**2.** cloudy		추운	**10.** cold
눈이 오는	**3.** snowy		몹시 추운	**11.** freezing
햇볕이 나는	**4.** sunny		안개 낀	**12.** foggy
온도계	**5.** thermometer		바람부는	**13.** windy
온도	**6.** temperature		건조한	**14.** dry
뜨거운	**7.** hot		젖은	**15.** wet
따뜻한	**8.** warm		얼음이 덮인	**16.** icy

계절에 관한 동사

봄	**Spring**	여름	**Summer**	가을	**Fall**	겨울	**Winter**
페인트 칠하다	**1.** paint	물주다	**5.** water	채우다	**9.** fill	눈 치우다	**13.** shovel
청소하다	**2.** clean	잔디 깎다	**6.** mow	긁어 모으다	**10.** rake	모래 뿌리다	**14.** sand
파다	**3.** dig	따다	**7.** pick	쪼개다	**11.** chop	긁어 벗기다	**15.** scrape
심다	**4.** plant	깎아 다듬다	**8.** trim	밀다	**12.** push	나르다	**16.** carry

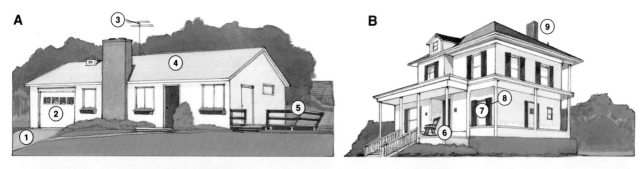

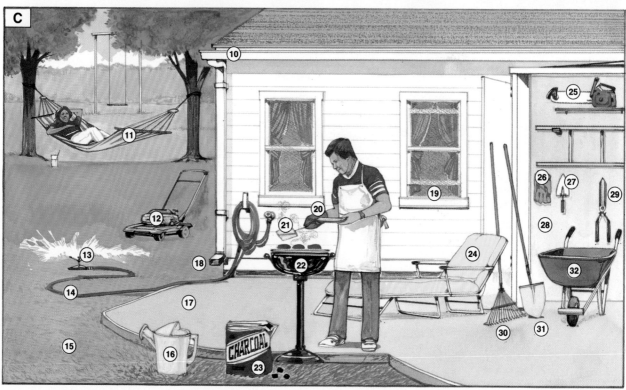

지붕의 경사가 완만한 단층식 주택 **A. Ranch House**

차도	1. driveway
차고	2. garage
텔레비젼 안테나	3. TV antenna
지붕	4. roof
집옆의 난간	5. deck

방이 여러개 있는 이층식 주택 **B. Colonial-style House**

현관	6. porch
창문	7. window
덧문	8. shutter
굴뚝	9. chimney

뒤뜰 **C. The Backyard**

처마 물받이	10. gutter
해먹	11. hammock
잔디 깎는 기계	12. lawn mower
물뿌리개	13. sprinkler
정원용 호스	14. garden hose

잔디	15. grass
손 물뿌리개	16. watering can
집의 안뜰	17. patio
배수관	18. drainpipe
방충망	19. screen
열 방지용 장갑	20. mitt
주걱	21. spatula
석쇠	22. grill
덩어리 연탄	23. charcoal briquettes
정원용 의자	24. lounge chair
전기 톱	25. power saw
작업용 장갑	26. work gloves
흙손	27. trowel
연장 헛간	28. toolshed
울타리 자르개	29. hedge clippers
갈퀴	30. rake
삽	31. shovel
외바퀴 손수레	32. wheelbarrow

천장 선풍기	**1.** ceiling fan	안락의자	**16.** recliner
천장	**2.** ceiling	원거리 조정기	**17.** remote control
벽	**3.** wall	텔레비전	**18.** television
틀	**4.** frame	벽 가구 셋트	**19.** wall unit
그림	**5.** painting	스테레오 건축	**20.** stereo system
화병	**6.** vase	스피커	**21.** speaker
덮개	**7.** mantel	책장	**22.** bookcase
벽난로	**8.** fireplace	커튼	**23.** drapes
불	**9.** fire	방석	**24.** cushion
통나무	**10.** log	소파	**25.** sofa
난간 동자	**11.** banister	커피 탁자	**26.** coffee table
계단 난간	**12.** staircase	조명등갓	**27.** lampshade
층계	**13.** step	조명등	**28.** lamp
책상	**14.** desk	작은 탁자	**29.** end table
양탄자	**15.** wall-to-wall carpeting		

도자기	**1.** china		식탁보	**16.** tablecloth
찬장	**2.** china closet		의자	**17.** chair
샹들리에	**3.** chandelier		커피 주전자	**18.** coffeepot
물주전자	**4.** pitcher		찻주전자	**19.** teapot
포도주 잔	**5.** wine glass		잔	**20.** cup
물 잔	**6.** water glass		받침 접시	**21.** saucer
식탁	**7.** table		식탁용 은제품	**22.** silverware
수저	**8.** spoon		설탕 그릇	**23.** sugar bowl
후추가루통	**9.** pepper shaker		크림 그릇	**24.** creamer
소금통	**10.** salt shaker		샐러드용 접시	**25.** salad bowl
빵을 놓는 접시	**11.** bread and butter plate		불꽃	**26.** flame
포크	**12.** fork		초	**27.** candle
접시	**13.** plate		촛대	**28.** candlestick
냅킨	**14.** napkin		찬장	**29.** buffet
나이프	**15.** knife			

접시 닦는 기계	**1.** dishwasher
물기 빼는 기구	**2.** dish drainer
찜통	**3.** steamer
깡통따개	**4.** can opener
프라이팬	**5.** frying pan
병따개	**6.** bottle opener
여과기	**7.** colander
수튜 남비	**8.** saucepan
뚜껑	**9.** lid
접시 닦기용 세제	**10.** dishwashing liquid
수세미	**11.** scouring pad
혼합기	**12.** blender
깊은 남비	**13.** pot
뚜껑있는 찜남비 그릇	**14.** casserole dish
차, 커피 통	**15.** canister
토스터	**16.** toaster
굽는 팬	**17.** roasting pan

접시 닦기용 행주	**18.** dish towel
냉장고	**19.** refrigerator
냉동실	**20.** freezer
얼음 제조대	**21.** ice tray
캐비넷	**22.** cabinet
전자 레인지	**23.** microwave oven
섞음용 그릇	**24.** mixing bowl
밀방망이	**25.** rolling pin
도마	**26.** cutting board
조리대	**27.** counter
차탕관	**28.** teakettle
연소기	**29.** burner
스토브	**30.** stove
커피 끓이는 기구	**31.** coffeemaker
오븐	**32.** oven
고기굽는 기구	**33.** broiler
남비집게	**34.** pot holder

부엌에서 요리할 때 쓰이는 동사

젓다	**1.** stir		자르다	**9.** cut
문지러 잘게 썰다	**2.** grate		얇게 썰다	**10.** slice
열다	**3.** open		토막내어 자르다	**11.** chop
쏟다	**4.** pour		찌다	**12.** steam
껍질을 벗기다	**5.** peel		불에 굽다	**13.** broil
고기 따위를 가르다	**6.** carve		직접 불에 대지 않고 굽다	**14.** bake
깨다	**7.** break		튀기다	**15.** fry
휘저어 섞다	**8.** beat		끓이다	**16.** boil

침실

걸쇠	**1.** hook	침대요	**17.** mattress
옷걸이	**2.** hanger	침대 스프링	**18.** box spring
옷장	**3.** closet	엷은 홑이불	**19.** (flat) sheet
보석함	**4.** jewelry box	담요	**20.** blanket
거울	**5.** mirror	침대	**21.** bed
빗	**6.** comb	이불	**22.** comforter
머리솔	**7.** hairbrush	침대커버	**23.** bedspread
자명종	**8.** alarm clock	침대 발판	**24.** footboard
거울 달린 옷장	**9.** bureau	전기 스위치	**25.** light switch
커튼	**10.** curtain	전화	**26.** phone
냉방장치	**11.** air conditioner	전화선	**a.** cord
차양	**12.** blinds	전화 플러그 꽂는 구멍	**b.** jack
화장지	**13.** tissues	침대곁 소형 책상	**27.** night table
침대 머리판	**14.** headboard	양탄자	**28.** rug
벼갯잇	**15.** pillowcase	바닥	**29.** floor
벼개	**16.** pillow	옷정리 장	**30.** chest of drawers

갓난 아기방

유리창 가리개	**1.** shade	고무 젖꼭지	**18.** nipple
움직이는 장난감	**2.** mobile	갓난아기용 위 아래가 딸린옷	**19.** stretchie
장난감 곰	**3.** teddy bear	턱받기	**20.** bib
둘레 난간이 있는 (소아용의) 침대	**4.** crib	딸랑이	**21.** rattle
완충대	**5.** bumper	고무 젖꼭지	**22.** pacifier
소아용 로숀	**6.** baby lotion	보행기	**23.** walker
소아용 분말	**7.** baby powder	그네	**24.** swing
소아용 닦음종이	**8.** baby wipes	인형 집	**25.** doll house
갈아 입히기용 책상	**9.** changing table	요람	**26.** cradle
목화 스왑	**10.** cotton swab	동물로 된 노리개	**27.** stuffed animal
안전핀	**11.** safety pin	인형	**28.** doll
일회용 기저귀	**12.** disposable diaper	장난감 보관함	**29.** toy chest
천 기저귀	**13.** cloth diaper	갓난아기의 놀이터	**30.** playpen
유모차	**14.** stroller	그림 맞추기	**31.** puzzle
연기 탐지기	**15.** smoke detector	장난감의 집짓기 토막	**32.** block
흔들이 의자	**16.** rocking chair	어린이용 변기	**33.** potty
젖병	**17.** bottle		

커튼 막대	**1.** curtain rod	더운 물 수도꼭지	**17.** hot water faucet
커튼 고리	**2.** curtain rings	찬 물 수도꼭지	**18.** cold water faucet
샤워 모자	**3.** shower cap	세면대	**19.** sink
샤워 머리	**4.** shower head	손톱솔	**20.** nailbrush
샤워장 커튼	**5.** shower curtain	치솔	**21.** toothbrush
비누 받이	**6.** soap dish	때밀이 수건	**22.** washcloth
스폰지	**7.** sponge	얼굴이나 손을 닦는 작은수건	**23.** hand towel
세발제	**8.** shampoo	몸 전체를 닦는 큰수건	**24.** bath towel
배수관	**9.** drain	수건걸이	**25.** towel rack
마개	**10.** stopper	머리 말리는 기계	**26.** hair dryer
욕조	**11.** bathtub	타일	**27.** tile
발 문지르개	**12.** bath mat	바구리	**28.** hamper
휴지통	**13.** wastepaper basket	변기	**29.** toilet
약상자	**14.** medicine chest	화장지	**30.** toilet paper
비누	**15.** soap	변기솔	**31.** toilet brush
치약	**16.** toothpaste	저울	**32.** scale

발판 사다리	**1.** stepladder	
먼지털이	**2.** feather duster	
회중전등	**3.** flashlight	
걸레	**4.** rags	
회로 차단기	**5.** circuit breaker	
(스폰지로 생긴) 자루걸레	**6.** (sponge) mop	
빗 자루	**7.** broom	
쓰레받기	**8.** dustpan	
세척제	**9.** cleanser	
창문 세척제	**10.** window cleaner	
갈음용 걸레	**11.** (mop) refill	
다리미	**12.** iron	
다림질판	**13.** ironing board	
흡입용 고무컵	**14.** plunger	
바께쓰	**15.** bucket	
진공 청소기	**16.** vacuum cleaner	

부속품	**17.** attachments
수도관	**18.** pipe
빨랫줄	**19.** clothesline
빨래 집게	**20.** clothespins
풀 뿌리게	**21.** spray starch
백열전구	**22.** lightbulb
종이 수건	**23.** paper towels
건조기계	**24.** dryer
세제	**25.** laundry detergent
표백제	**26.** bleach
연화제	**27.** fabric softener
세탁물	**28.** laundry
세탁용 바구리	**29.** laundry basket
세탁기	**30.** washing machine
쓰레기통	**31.** garbage can
쥐 덫	**32.** mousetrap

작업장

접자	**1.** carpenter's rule	망치	**13.** hammer
죔쇠	**2.** C-clamp	문지르는 도구	**14.** scraper
실톱(곡선으로 켜는데 씀)	**3.** jigsaw	연장 걸이대	**15.** pegboard
나무(판자)	**4.** wood	걸이	**16.** hook
연장선	**5.** extension cord	손도끼	**17.** hatchet
배출구	**6.** outlet	금속용 쇠톱	**18.** hacksaw
지면 플러그	**7.** grounding plug	뺀찌	**19.** pliers
톱	**8.** saw	둥근 톱	**20.** circular saw
타래송곳	**9.** brace	줄자	**21.** tape measure
렌치	**10.** wrench	작업대	**22.** workbench
나무메	**11.** mallet	연장통	**23.** toolbox
멍키 렌치	**12.** monkey wrench		

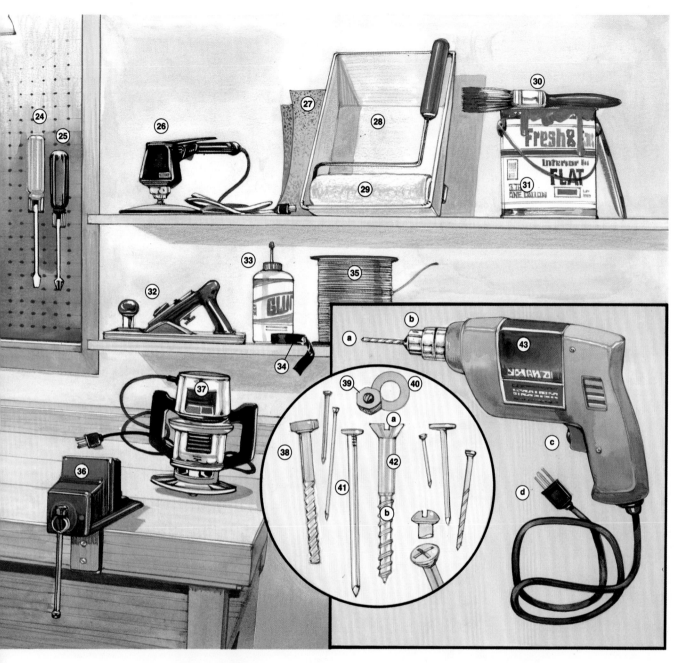

나사돌리개	**24.** screwdriver	루터 (철·나무를 짜르는 대패의 일종)		**37.** router
네모 나사돌리개	**25.** Phillips screwdriver	나사못		**38.** bolt
전원함	**26.** power sander	고정 나사		**39.** nut
샌드페이퍼	**27.** sandpaper	똬리쇠		**40.** washer
롤러팬	**28.** pan	못		**41.** nail
롤러	**29.** roller	나사		**42.** screw
페인트솔	**30.** paintbrush	나사머리		**a.** head
페인트	**31.** paint	나사산		**b.** thread
대패	**32.** wood plane	전기 송곳		**43.** electric drill
접착제	**33.** glue	날		**a.** bit
전기 테이프	**34.** electrical tape	대		**b.** shank
철사	**35.** wire	스위치		**c.** switch
죄임 기계	**36.** vise	플러그		**d.** plug

집안일과 수선하는데 쓰이는 동사

집다	**1.** fold	닦아내다	**9.** dry
문지르다	**2.** scrub	수선하다	**10.** repair
윤을 내다	**3.** polish	다리미질하다	**11.** iron
조이다	**4.** tighten	기름을 치다	**12.** oil
닦아내다	**5.** wipe	갈아끼우다	**13.** change (the sheets)
걸다	**6.** hang	진공 청소기로 청소하다	**14.** vacuum
쓸다	**7.** sweep	먼지를 털다	**15.** dust
잠자리를 짤다(개다)	**8.** make (the bed)	씻다	**16.** wash

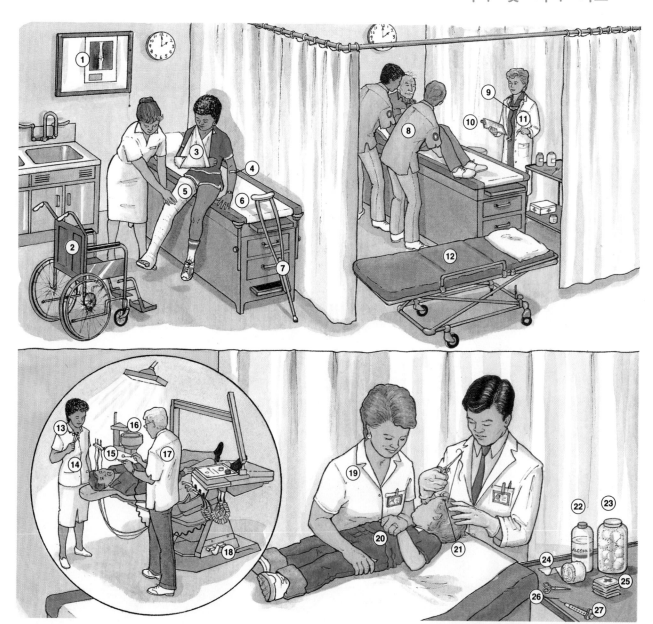

엑스선	1. X-ray	천공기	15. drill
바퀴 달린 의자	2. wheelchair	물통	16. basin
삼각봉대	3. sling	치과의사	17. dentist
일회용 반창고	4. Band-Aid	발판	18. pedal
깁스봉대	5. cast	간호원	19. nurse
진찰대	6. examining table	환자	20. patient
목발	7. crutch	상처를 꿰맨 바늘 뜸	21. stitches
보조원	8. attendant	알콜	22. alcohol
청진기	9. stethoscope	솜 덩어리	23. cotton balls
차트	10. chart	붕대	24. (gauze) bandage
의사	11. doctor	가제 패드	25. gauze pads
누임용 침대	12. stretcher	주사바늘	26. needle
기구	13. instruments	주사기	27. syringe
구강 위생기사	14. oral hygienist		

가벼운 질병 및 상처

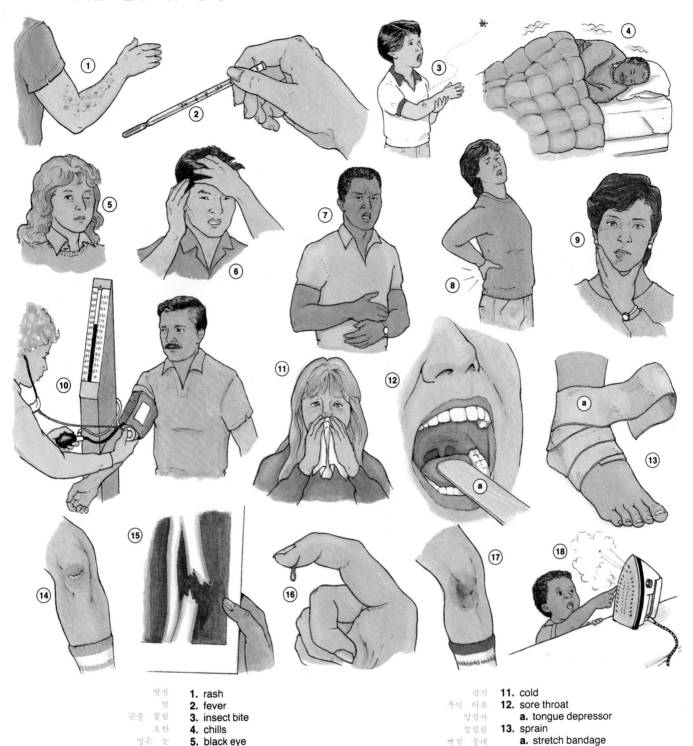

발진	**1.** rash	감기	**11.** cold
열	**2.** fever	목이 아픔	**12.** sore throat
곤충 물림	**3.** insect bite	압설자	**a.** tongue depressor
오한	**4.** chills	접질림	**13.** sprain
멍든 눈	**5.** black eye	뻗힘 붕대	**a.** stretch bandage
두통	**6.** headache	감염	**14.** infection
위통	**7.** stomachache	절골	**15.** broken bone
요통	**8.** backache	베인 상처	**16.** cut
치통	**9.** toothache	타박상	**17.** bruise
고혈압	**10.** high blood pressure	화상	**18.** burn

치 료 및 구 제 법

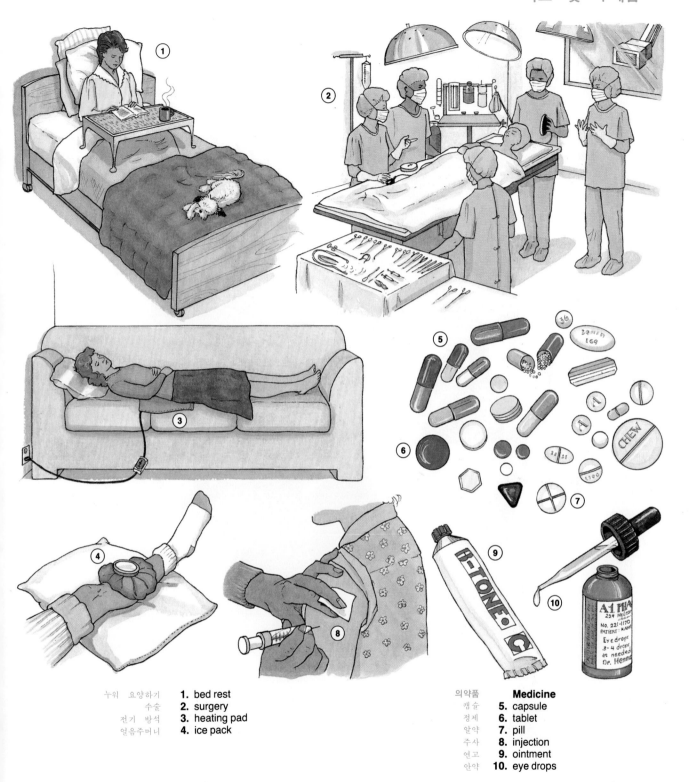

누워 요양하기	**1.** bed rest
수술	**2.** surgery
전기 방석	**3.** heating pad
얼음주머니	**4.** ice pack

의약품	**Medicine**
캡슐	**5.** capsule
정제	**6.** tablet
알약	**7.** pill
주사	**8.** injection
연고	**9.** ointment
안약	**10.** eye drops

진화 작업 및 구조

사다리	**1.** ladder		소방수	**10.** fire fighter
소방 펌프	**2.** fire engine		소화기	**11.** fire extinguisher
소방차	**3.** fire truck		헬멧	**12.** helmet
비상구	**4.** fire escape		외투	**13.** coat
화재	**5.** fire		도끼	**14.** ax
구급차	**6.** ambulance		연기	**15.** smoke
준의료 활동원	**7.** paramedic		물	**16.** water
호스	**8.** hose		호스 주둥이	**17.** nozzle
소화전	**9.** fire hydrant			

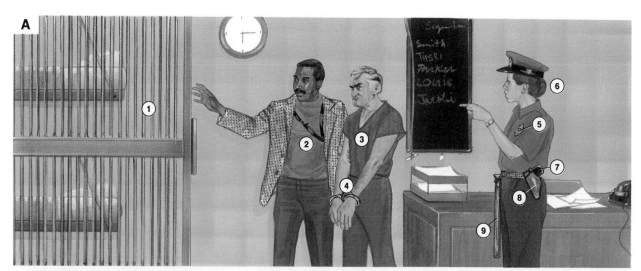

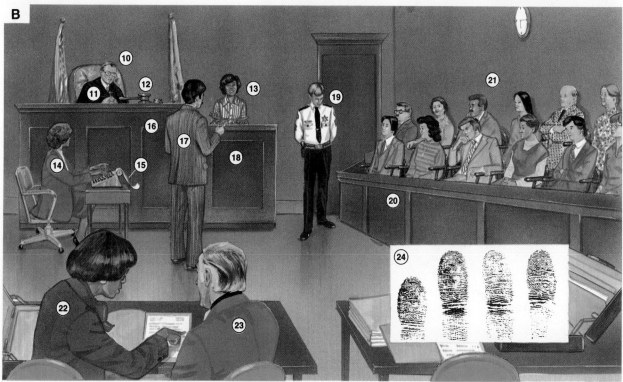

경찰서	**A. Police Station**
감옥	**1.** jail
형사	**2.** detective
현의자	**3.** suspect
수갑	**4.** handcuffs
휘장	**5.** badge
경찰관	**6.** police officer
권총	**7.** gun
권총용 가죽지갑	**8.** holster
야경봉	**9.** nightstick
법원	**B. Court**
판사	**10.** judge
재판관의 법복	**11.** robes

사회봉	**12.** gavel
증인	**13.** witness
법원 서기	**14.** court reporter
법정 기록서	**15.** transcript
판사석	**16.** bench
검찰관	**17.** prosecuting attorney
증인석	**18.** witness stand
법원 경찰관	**19.** court officer
배심원석	**20.** jury box
배심원	**21.** jury
피고측 변호사	**22.** defense attorney
피고	**23.** defendant
지문	**24.** fingerprints

사무실용 큰 빌딩	**1.** office building
로비	**2.** lobby
길 모퉁이	**3.** corner
횡단보도	**4.** crosswalk
백화점	**5.** department store
제과점	**6.** bakery
공중전화	**7.** public telephone
도로표지	**8.** street sign

우체국	**9.** post office
교통 경찰관	**10.** traffic cop
네거리	**11.** intersection
보행자	**12.** pedestrian
버스 정류장	**13.** bus stop
긴 의자	**14.** bench
쓰레기통	**15.** trash basket
지하철 역	**16.** subway station

승강기	**17.** elevator	보도	**25.** sidewalk
서점	**18.** bookstore	도로가	**26.** curb
주차장	**19.** parking garage	유모차	**27.** baby carriage
주차시간 자동표시기	**20.** parking meter	청과물 시장	**28.** fruit and vegetable market
교통 신호등	**21.** traffic light	가로등	**29.** streetlight
약국	**22.** drugstore	신문 판매점	**30.** newsstand
아파트	**23.** apartment house	거리	**31.** street
건물 번호	**24.** building number	잠입구	**32.** manhole

미국 우편국 제도

우편물 배달	**A. Delivering Mail**
우체통	1. mailbox
우편물	2. mail
우체부	3. letter carrier
우편 배달용 가방	4. mailbag
우편 배달용 트럭	5. mail truck
미국 우체통	6. U.S. mailbox
편지	7. letter
발신인의 주소·성명	8. return address
소인	9. postmark
우표	10. stamp
주소	11. address
우편번호	12. zip code

우체국	**B. The Post Office**
우편물 넣는 긴 구멍	13. mail slot
우체국원	14. postal worker
창구	15. window

우편물 종류	**C. Types of Mail**
항공 우편봉투	16. (airmail) envelope
우편엽서	17. postcard
송금환	18. money order
소포	19. package
줄	20. string
레이블	21. label
테이프	22. tape
속달 우편	23. Express Mail (package)

SUBJECT

332-346
347-369

370-422
423-574

575-613
614-623

624-702
703-74_

972   Bridenbaugh, Carl
Early Americans
294 p   1981   History-US

AMERICAN
JOURNAL
1940-1950

INFORMATION

사시	**1.** library clerk
접수처	**2.** checkout desk
도서관 증	**3.** library card
카드식 목록	**4.** card catalog
서랍	**5.** drawer
분류표	**6.** call card
분류 번호	**7.** call number
저자	**8.** author
제목	**9.** title
주제	**10.** subject
열	**11.** row
열람표	**12.** call slip
마이크로필름	**13.** microfilm

마이크로필름 판독기	**14.** microfilm reader
정기간행물 구역	**15.** periodicals section
잡지	**16.** magazine
책 진열대	**17.** rack
복사기	**18.** photocopy machine
지구본	**19.** globe
지도책	**20.** atlas
참고 목록 구역	**21.** reference section
안내처	**22.** information desk
사서	**23.** (reference) librarian
사전	**24.** dictionary
백과사전	**25.** encyclopedia
책꽂이	**26.** shelf

군대 : 육 · 해 · 공군

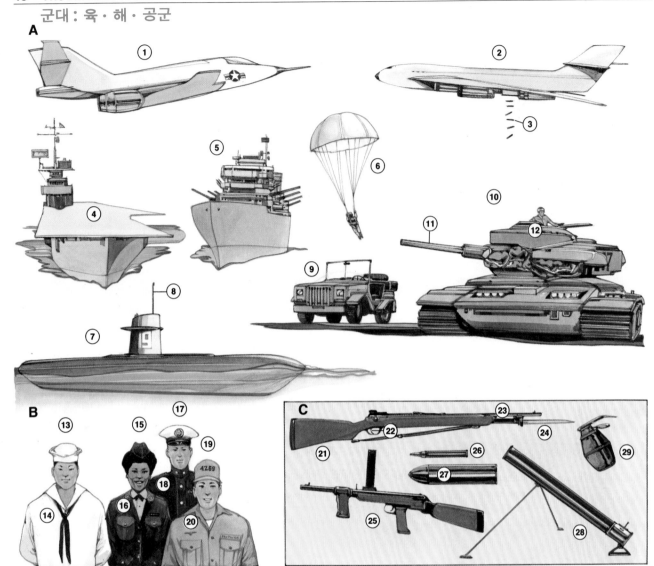

	A. Vehicles and Equipment
탈것 및 장비	**A. Vehicles and Equipment**
전투기	**1.** fighter plane
폭격기	**2.** bomber
폭탄	**3.** bomb
항공 모함	**4.** aircraft carrier
전투함	**5.** battleship
낙하산	**6.** parachute
잠수함	**7.** submarine
잠망경	**8.** periscope
지프	**9.** jeep
탱크	**10.** tank
대포	**11.** cannon
총포탑	**12.** gun turret

	B. Personnel
인사조직	**B. Personnel**
해군	**13.** Navy
수병	**14.** sailor

육군	**15.** Army
군인	**16.** soldier
해병대	**17.** Marines
해병	**18.** marine
공군	**19.** Air Force
항공병	**20.** airman

	C. Weapons and Ammunition
무기 및 탄약	**C. Weapons and Ammunition**
소총	**21.** rifle
방아쇠	**22.** trigger
총열	**23.** barrel
총검	**24.** bayonet
기관총	**25.** machine gun
탄알	**26.** bullet
탄피	**27.** shell
박격포	**28.** mortar
수류탄	**29.** hand grenade

거리 청소차	**1.** street cleaner
견인차	**2.** tow truck
연료차	**3.** fuel truck
용달차	**4.** pickup truck
제설차	**5.** snow plow
쓰레기차	**6.** garbage truck
청소부	**7.** sanitation worker
포장마차	**8.** lunch truck
소형 화물차	**9.** panel truck

배달부	**10.** delivery person
이삿짐 운반차	**11.** moving van
운송업자	**12.** mover
시멘트 트럭	**13.** cement truck
덤프 트럭	**14.** dump truck
견인 트레일러	**15.** tractor trailer
트럭 운전수	**16.** truck driver
차운반용 대형 트럭	**17.** transporter
수평식 트레일러	**18.** flatbed

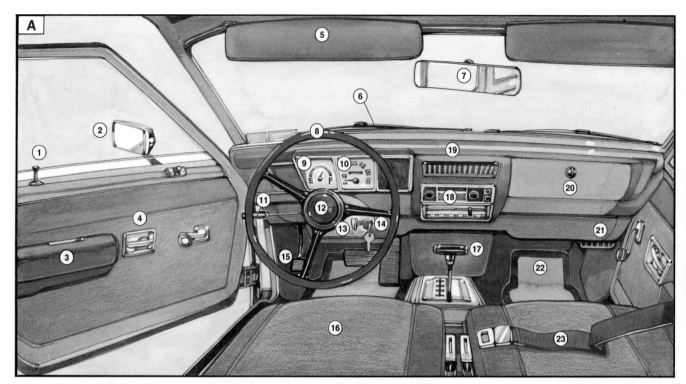

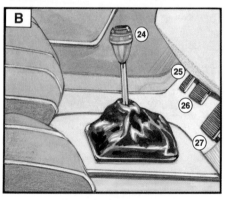

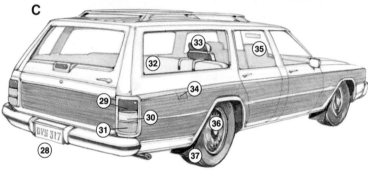

자동식 변속장치	**A. Automatic Transmission**
차문 자물쇠	**1.** door lock
자동차의 옆 거울	**2.** side mirror
팔걸이	**3.** armrest
문 손잡이	**4.** door handle
차양판	**5.** visor
창문 눈·비 닦개	**6.** windshield wiper
백미러	**7.** rearview mirror
핸들	**8.** steering wheel
가스 게이지	**9.** gas gauge
속도계	**10.** speedometer
방향 지시 지레	**11.** turn signal lever
경적	**12.** horn
둥근 몸통	**13.** column
점화장치	**14.** ignition
사이드 브레이크	**15.** emergency brake
접의자(1인용)	**16.** bucket seat
변속지레	**17.** gearshift
라디오	**18.** radio
계기판	**19.** dashboard
잡물통	**20.** glove compartment

환기 구멍	**21.** vent
매트	**22.** mat
좌석 벨트	**23.** seat belt
수동식 변속장치	**B. Manual Transmission**
기어 변환 레버	**24.** stick shift
전동장치	**25.** clutch
제동기	**26.** brake
가속장치	**27.** accelerator
스테이션 왜건	**C. Station Wagon**
번호판	**28.** license plate
브레이크등	**29.** brake light
후진등	**30.** back-up light
미등	**31.** taillight
뒷좌석	**32.** backseat
유아석	**33.** child's seat
가스탱크	**34.** gas tank
머리 받침	**35.** headrest
휠캡	**36.** hubcap
타이어	**37.** tire

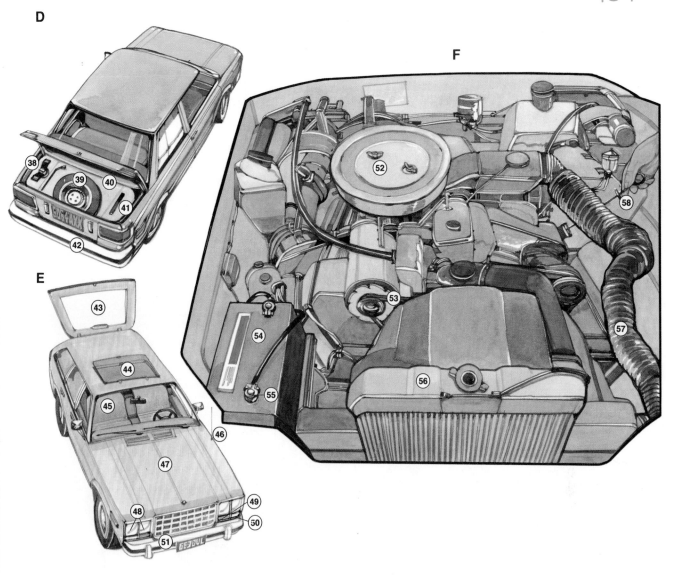

D

E

F

2 중문 세단	**D. (Two-door) Sedan**
밀어 올리는 기계	**38.** jack
예비 타이어	**39.** spare tire
트렁크	**40.** trunk
플레어	**41.** flare
뒤범바	**42.** rear bumper

4 중문 해치백	**E. Four-door Hatchback**
해치백	**43.** hatchback
개폐식 천장달린 지붕	**44.** sunroof
바람막이 유리	**45.** windshield
공중선	**46.** antenna
엔진 뚜껑	**47.** hood

헤드라이트	**48.** headlights
주차등	**49.** parking lights
방향 지시등	**50.** turn signal (lights)
앞 범바	**51.** front bumper

엔진	**F. Engine**
공기 여과기	**52.** air filter
팬 벨트	**53.** fan belt
충전지	**54.** battery
터미널 (전기선의 끝 연결 부분)	**55.** terminal
라디에이터	**56.** radiator
호스	**57.** hose
계심봉	**58.** dipstick

자전거

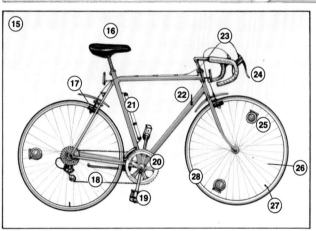

훈련용 바퀴	**1.** training wheels	사슬	**18.** chain
핸들	**2.** (racing) handlebars	페달	**19.** pedal
여학생용 중앙 버팀쇠	**3.** girl's frame	사슬바퀴	**20.** sprocket
바퀴	**4.** wheel	펌프	**21.** pump
경적	**5.** horn	기어 변속기	**22.** gear changer
세발 자전거	**6.** tricycle	케이블	**23.** cable
헬멧	**7.** helmet	수동 브레이크	**24.** hand brake
흙투성이의 자전거	**8.** dirt bike	반사물기	**25.** reflector
뒷받침 살	**9.** kickstand	바퀴의 살	**26.** spoke
바퀴 덮개	**10.** fender	밸브	**27.** valve
남학생용 중앙 버팀쇠	**11.** boy's frame	타이어	**28.** tire
조종 핸들	**12.** touring handlebars	스쿠터	**29.** motor scooter
자물쇠	**13.** lock	오토바이	**30.** motorcycle
자전거 세우는 곳	**14.** bike stand	완충기	**31.** shock absorbers
자전거	**15.** bicycle	엔진	**32.** engine
안장	**16.** seat	배기관	**33.** exhaust pipe
제동기	**17.** brake		

주간 고속도로	**1.** interstate highway
출구 램프	**2.** exit ramp
육교	**3.** overpass
입체 교차로	**4.** cloverleaf
좌측선	**5.** left lane
중앙선	**6.** center lane
우측선	**7.** right lane
속도 제한 표시	**8.** speed limit sign
자동차 편승 여행자	**9.** hitchhiker
트레일러	**10.** trailer
휴게소	**11.** service area
점원	**12.** attendant
공기 펌프	**13.** air pump
가솔린 펌프	**14.** gas pump

승용차	**15.** passenger car
캠프용 트레일러	**16.** camper
스포츠카	**17.** sports car
중앙 분리대	**18.** center divider
오토바이	**19.** motorcycle
버스	**20.** bus
입구 램프	**21.** entrance ramp
도로와 땅의 연결부	**22.** shoulder
도로표지	**23.** road sign
출구표지	**24.** exit sign
트럭	**25.** truck
봉고차	**26.** van
통행세 징수소	**27.** tollbooth

공공 운송기관

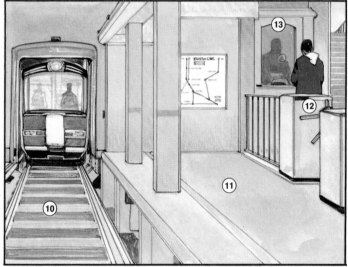

버스	**A. Bus**		지하철	**B. Subway**
정지선	**1.** cord		차장	**7.** conductor
좌석	**2.** seat		손잡이	**8.** strap
버스 운전수	**3.** bus driver		칸	**9.** car
갈아 타는표	**4.** transfer		궤도	**10.** track
요금함	**5.** fare box		승강단	**11.** platform
승객	**6.** rider		십자형 회전식 문	**12.** turnstile
			토큰 파는곳	**13.** token booth

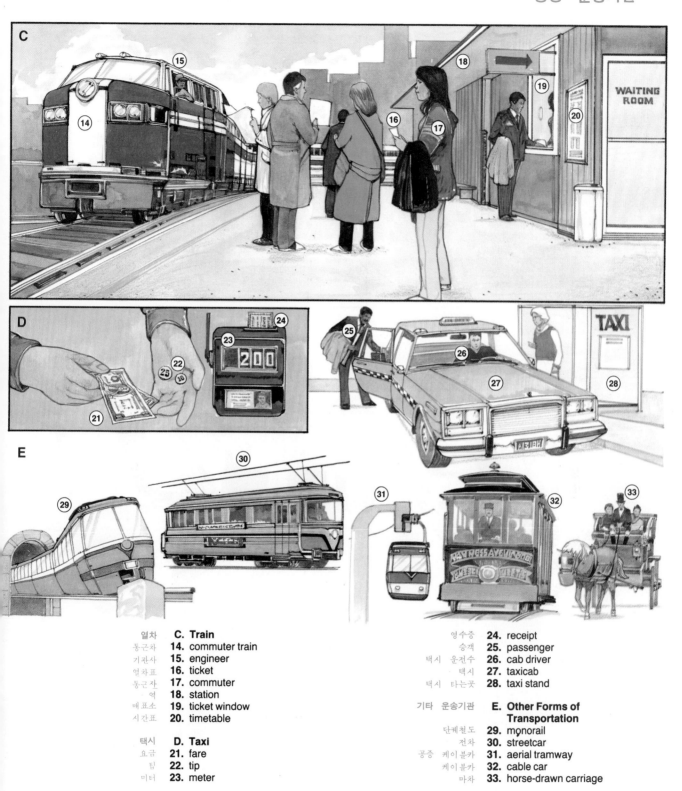

열차	**C. Train**
통근차	**14.** commuter train
기관사	**15.** engineer
열차표	**16.** ticket
통근자	**17.** commuter
역	**18.** station
매표소	**19.** ticket window
시간표	**20.** timetable

택시	**D. Taxi**
요금	**21.** fare
팁	**22.** tip
미터	**23.** meter

영수증	**24.** receipt
승객	**25.** passenger
택시 운전수	**26.** cab driver
택시	**27.** taxicab
택시 타는곳	**28.** taxi stand

기타 운송기관	**E. Other Forms of Transportation**
단궤철도	**29.** monorail
전차	**30.** streetcar
공중 케이블카	**31.** aerial tramway
케이블카	**32.** cable car
마차	**33.** horse-drawn carriage

항공 여행

공항 체크인	Airport Check-In
의복용 가방	1. garment bag
휴대용 가방	2. carry-on bag
여행자	3. traveler
비행기표	4. ticket
운반인	5. porter
손수레	6. dolly
여행가방	7. suitcase
수화물	8. baggage

보안조치	Security
경비원	9. security guard
금속 탐지기	10. metal detector
엑스선 영상면	11. X-ray screener
이동 벨트	12. conveyor belt

탑승	Boarding
조종실	13. cockpit
계기	14. instruments
조종사	15. pilot
부조종사	16. copilot
항공 기관사	17. flight engineer
탑승권	18. boarding pass
객실	19. cabin
승무원	20. flight attendant
여행자 휴대품 넣는 함	21. luggage compartment
좌석에 붙은 음식 받침대	22. tray table
통로	23. aisle

A

B

항공기 종류	**A. Aircraft Types**
열기 풍선	**1.** hot air balloon
헬리콥터	**2.** helicopter
회전익	**a.** rotor
개인 전용 비행기	**3.** private jet
글라이더	**4.** glider
소형 비행선	**5.** blimp
행글라이더	**6.** hang glider
프로펠러 추진 비행기	**7.** propeller plane
코	**8.** nose
날개	**9.** wing
꼬리	**10.** tail

이륙	**B. Takeoff**
제트 엔진	**11.** jet engine
화물실	**12.** cargo area
화물실 문	**13.** cargo door
기체	**14.** fuselage
착륙 장치	**15.** landing gear
터미날 건물	**16.** terminal building
격납고	**17.** hangar
제트 비행기	**18.** (jet) plane
활주로	**19.** runway
관제탑	**20.** control tower

어선	**1.** fishing boat		부표	**16.** buoy
어부	**2.** fisherman		연락선	**17.** ferry
부두	**3.** pier		굴뚝	**18.** smokestack
포크리프트	**4.** forklift		구조선	**19.** lifeboat
뱃머리	**5.** bow		하역구	**20.** gangway
기중기	**6.** crane		창구	**21.** porthole
콘테이너	**7.** container		갑판	**22.** deck
배밑의 선창	**8.** hold		닻줄통	**23.** windlass
화물선	**9.** (container)ship		닻	**24.** anchor
화물	**10.** cargo		밧줄	**25.** line
선미	**11.** stern		계선주	**26.** bollard
바닥이 평평한 짐 배	**12.** barge		원양 여객선	**27.** ocean liner
예인선	**13.** tugboat		계선장	**28.** dock
등대	**14.** lighthouse		터미날	**29.** terminal
유조선	**15.** tanker			

구명복	**1.** life jacket
카누	**2.** canoe
노	**3.** paddle
돛배	**4.** sailboat
키	**5.** rudder
이동 용골	**6.** centerboard
돛의 아래 활대	**7.** boom
돛대	**8.** mast
돛	**9.** sail
수상 스키하는 사람	**10.** water-skier
끄는 밧줄	**11.** towrope
선외 발동기	**12.** outboard motor

발동기선	**13.** motorboat
윈드서핑하는 사람	**14.** windsurfer
1 - 2인용 소형 요트	**15.** sailboard
행락용 모터 보우트	**16.** cabin cruiser
카약(카누형보트)	**17.** kayak
상륙용 작은 배	**18.** dinghy
계류 장치	**19.** mooring
압축용 고무 보트	**20.** inflatable raft
노받이	**21.** oarlock
노	**22.** oar
노로 젓는 배	**23.** rowboat

식물 및 나무

꽃	**Flowers**		치자나무	**14.** gardenia
튤립	**1.** tulip		홍성초	**15.** poinsettia
줄기	**a.** stem		제비꽃	**16.** violet
팬지	**2.** pansy		미나리아재비	**17.** buttercup
백합	**3.** lily		장미	**18.** rose
국화	**4.** (chrysanthe)mum		봉오리	**a.** bud
데이지	**5.** daisy		꽃잎	**b.** petal
금잔화속의 식물	**6.** marigold		가시	**c.** thorn
피튜니어	**7.** petunia		해바라기	**19.** sunflower
나팔수선화	**8.** daffodil			
구근	**a.** bulb		풀과 곡류	**Grasses and Grains**
크로커스	**9.** crocus		사탕수수	**20.** sugarcane
허아신스	**10.** hyacinth		모판 벼	**21.** rice
붓꽃	**11.** iris		밀	**22.** wheat
난초	**12.** orchid		귀리	**23.** oats
백일초	**13.** zinnia		옥수수	**24.** corn

나무	**Trees**		느릅나무	**36.** elm
미국 삼나무	**25.** redwood		잎사귀	**a.** leaf
종려	**26.** palm		호랑가시나무	**37.** holly
유칼립투스	**27.** eucalyptus		단풍나무	**38.** maple
말채나무	**28.** dogwood			
목련	**29.** magnolia		기타 식물	**Other Plants**
포플라	**30.** poplar		실내 화분 식물	**39.** house plants
버드나무	**31.** willow		선인장	**40.** cactus
자작나무	**32.** birch		수풀	**41.** bushes
참나무	**33.** oak		덩굴	**42.** vine
잔가지	**a.** twig			
도토리	**b.** acorn		유독식물	**Poisonous Plants**
소나무	**34.** pine		덩굴 옻나무 (오크)	**43.** poison oak
솔잎	**a.** needle		옻나무	**44.** poison sumac
솔방울	**b.** cone		덩굴 옻나무 (아이비)	**45.** poison ivy
나무	**35.** tree			
가지	**a.** branch			
줄기	**b.** trunk			
나무껍질	**c.** bark			
뿌리	**d.** root			

간단한 동물

달팽이	**1.** snail
껍질	**a.** shell
더듬이	**b.** antenna
굴	**2.** oyster
홍합	**3.** mussel
팔태충	**4.** slug
오징어	**5.** squid
문어	**6.** octopus
불가사리	**7.** starfish

새우	**8.** shrimp
게	**9.** crab
가리비	**10.** scallop
벌레 (지렁이 · 모충등)	**11.** worm
해파리	**12.** jellyfish
촉수	**a.** tentacle
바닷가재	**13.** lobster
집게발	**a.** claw

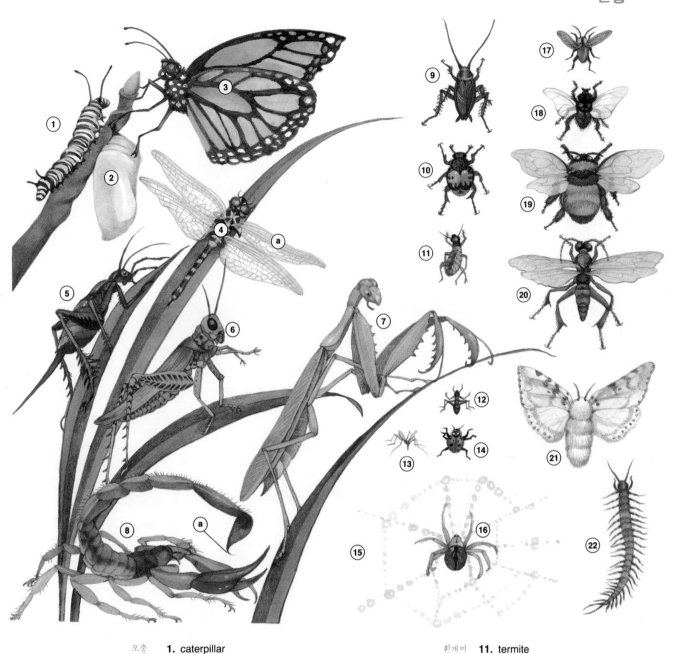

모충	**1.** caterpillar	흰개미	**11.** termite
고치	**2.** cocoon	개미	**12.** ant
나비	**3.** butterfly	모기	**13.** mosquito
잠자리	**4.** dragonfly	무당벌레	**14.** ladybug
날개	**a.** wing	거미집	**15.** web
귀뚜라미	**5.** cricket	거미	**16.** spider
메뚜기	**6.** grasshopper	개똥벌레	**17.** firefly
버마재비	**7.** mantis	파리	**18.** fly
전갈	**8.** scorpion	벌	**19.** bee
침	**a.** sting	장수말벌	**20.** wasp
바퀴벌레	**9.** cockroach	나방	**21.** moth
딱정벌레	**10.** beetle	지네	**22.** centipede

새

비둘기	**1.** pigeon		앵무새	**16.** parrot
날개	**a.** wing		딱다구리	**17.** woodpecker
벌새	**2.** hummingbird		공작새	**18.** peacock
까마귀	**3.** crow		꿩	**19.** pheasant
부리	**a.** beak		칠면조	**20.** turkey
갈매기	**4.** sea gull		수닭	**21.** rooster
독수리	**5.** eagle		병아리	**22.** chick
부엉이	**6.** owl		닭	**23.** chicken
매	**7.** hawk		펠리컨	**24.** pelican
깃털	**a.** feather		부리	**a.** bill
블루제이 (어치의 일종)	**8.** blue jay		집오리	**25.** duck
울새	**9.** robin		거위	**26.** goose
참새	**10.** sparrow		펭귄	**27.** penguin
홍관조	**11.** cardinal		백조	**28.** swan
타조	**12.** ostrich		플라밍고	**29.** flamingo
알	**13.** egg		황새	**30.** stork
카나리아	**14.** canary		둥우리	**31.** nest
잉꼬	**15.** parakeet		북미 남서부산 새 (뻐꾸기와 비슷함)	**32.** roadrunner

물고기 및 파충류

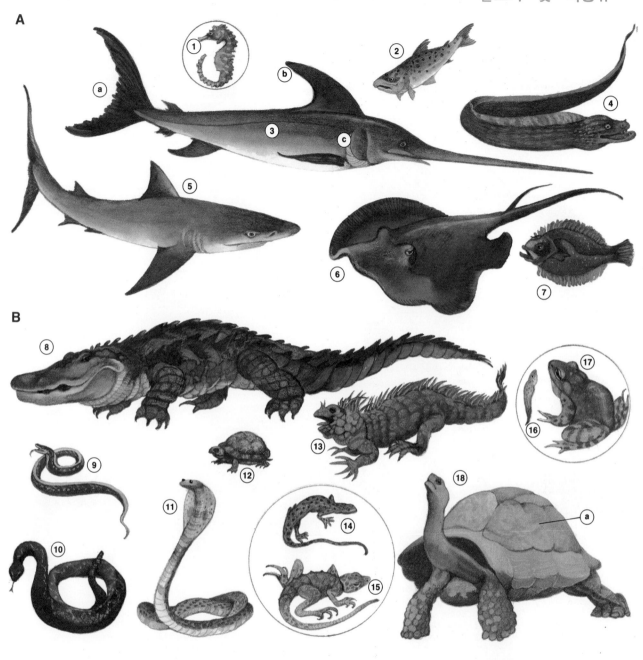

A

B

물고기	**A. Fish**
해마	**1.** sea horse
송어	**2.** trout
황새치	**3.** swordfish
꼬리	**a.** tail
지느러미	**b.** fin
아가미	**c.** gill
뱀장어	**4.** eel
상어	**5.** shark
가오리	**6.** stingray
넙치류	**7.** flounder

양서류 및 파충류	**B. Amphibians and Reptiles**
악어	**8.** alligator
뱀	**9.** (garter) snake
방울뱀	**10.** rattlesnake
코브라	**11.** cobra
바다거북	**12.** turtle
초식성 큰 도마뱀	**13.** iguana
불도마뱀	**14.** salamander
도마뱀	**15.** lizard
올챙이	**16.** tadpole
개구리	**17.** frog
거북	**18.** tortoise
등딱지	**a.** shell

복대가 있거나 이가 없거나 또는
날아 다니는 포유동물
새끼를 업고 다니는 곰

Pouched, Toothless, or Flying Mammals

빈치목   1. koala
캥거루   2. armadillo
꼬리   3. kangaroo
뒷다리   a. tail
복대   b. hind legs
앞다리   c. pouch
박쥐   d. forelegs
개미핥기   4. bat
            5. anteater

같는동물   **Rodents**
얼룩다람쥐   6. chipmunk
쥐   7. rat
들다람쥐   8. gopher

생쥐   9. mouse
다람쥐   10. squirrel
호저   11. porcupine
가시   a. quill
비버   12. beaver
토끼   13. rabbit

발굽있는 포유동물   **Hoofed Mammals**
하마   14. hippopotamus
아메리카낙타   15. llama
코뿔소   16. rhinoceros
뿔   a. horn
코끼리   17. elephant
코   a. trunk
엄니   b. tusk
얼룩말   18. zebra

둘소	**19.** bison			기린	**29.** giraffe
조랑말	**20.** pony			돼지	**30.** hog
말	**21.** horse			송아지	**31.** calf
머리털	**a.** mane			암소	**32.** cow
망아지	**22.** foal			낙타	**33.** camel
당나귀	**23.** donkey			혹	**a.** hump
어린양	**24.** lamb			황소	**34.** bull
면양	**25.** sheep			큰사슴	**35.** moose
사슴	**26.** deer			뿔	**a.** antler
새끼사슴	**27.** fawn			발굽	**b.** hoof
염소	**28.** goat				

표범	**1.** leopard	물에서 사는 포유동물	**Aquatic Mammals**
호랑이	**2.** tiger	고래	**9.** whale
발톱	**a.** claw	수달	**10.** otter
사자	**3.** lion	해마	**11.** walrus
고양이	**4.** cat	바다표범	**12.** seal
새끼고양이	**5.** kitten	물갈퀴	**a.** flipper
여우	**6.** fox	돌고래	**13.** dolphin
미국 너구리	**7.** raccoon		
스컹크	**8.** skunk		

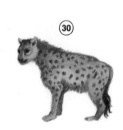

영장류	**Primates**		개	**Dogs**
원숭이	**14.** monkey	털의 결이 곱고 귀가 긴 개	**24.** spaniel
긴팔 원숭이	**15.** gibbon	애완견	**25.** terrier
침팬지	**16.** chimpanzee	사냥개	**26.** retriever
고릴라	**17.** gorilla	강아지	**27.** puppy
오랑우탄	**18.** orangutan	양치기 개	**28.** shepherd
비비	**19.** baboon	늑대	**29.** wolf
		발	**a.** paw
곰	**Bears**	하이에나	**30.** hyena
흑백곰	**20.** panda		
흑곰	**21.** black bear		
북극곰	**22.** polar bear		
회색의 큰곰	**23.** grizzly bear		

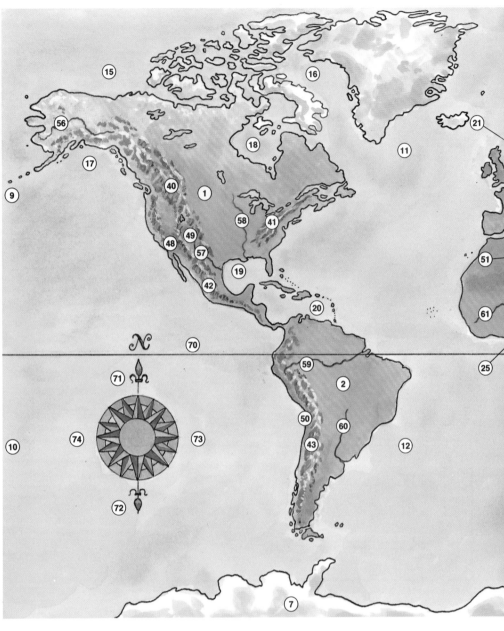

대륙	**Continents**	인도양	13. Indian	흑해	26. Black Sea
북미	1. North America	남극해	14. Antarctic	캐스피언해	27. Caspian Sea
남미	2. South America			페르시아만	28. Persian Gulf
유럽	3. Europe	바다와 만	**Seas, Gulfs, and Bays**	홍해	29. Red Sea
아프리카	4. Africa	보퍼드 해	15. Beaufort Sea	아라비아해	30. Arabian Sea
아시아	5. Asia	배핀 만	16. Baffin Bay	카라해	31. Kara Sea
오스트레일리아	6. Australia	알라스카 만	17. Gulf of Alaska	뱅갈만	32. Bay of Bengal
남극	7. Antarctica	허드슨 만	18. Hudson Bay	랍테 브해	33. Laptev Sea
		멕시코 만	19. Gulf of Mexico	베어링해	34. Bering Sea
대양	**Oceans**	카리브 해	20. Caribbean Sea	오호츠크해	35. Sea of Okhotsk
북극	8. Arctic	북해	21. North Sea	일본해	36. Sea of Japan
북태평양	9. North Pacific	발트해	22. Baltic Sea	황해	37. Yellow Sea
남태평양	10. South Pacific	베렌츠 해	23. Barents Sea	동지나해	38. East China Sea
북대서양	11. North Atlantic	지중해	24. Mediterranean Sea	남지 나해	39. South China Sea
남대서양	12. South Atlantic	기니아 만	25. Gulf of Guinea		

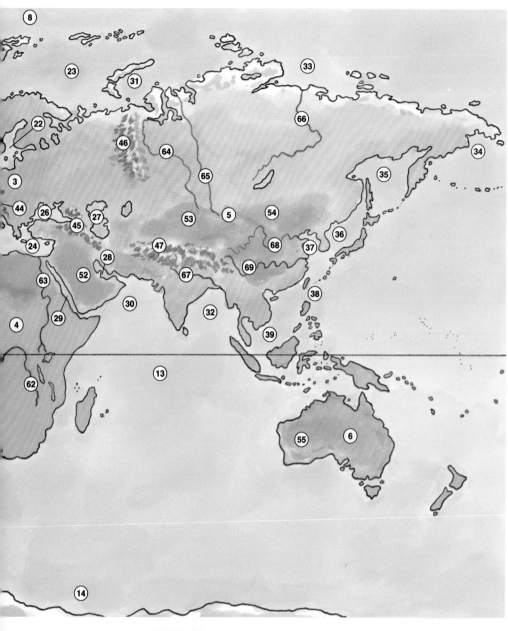

산맥		**Mountain Ranges**		사하라 사막	**51.** Sahara	나일 강	**63.** Nile

	산맥	**Mountain Ranges**	사하라 사막	**51.** Sahara	나일 강	**63.** Nile
록키	산맥	**40.** Rocky Mountains	러브알 칼리 사막	**52.** Rub' al Khali	오비 강	**64.** Ob
아팔라치언	산맥	**41.** Appalachian Mountains	탁라 마칸 사막	**53.** Takla Makan	예니세이 강	**65.** Yenisey
시에라마드레	산맥	**42.** Sierra Madre	고비사막	**54.** Gobi	니나 강	**66.** Lena
안데스	산맥	**43.** Andes	그레이트 샌디 사막	**55.** Great Sandy	간지스 강	**67.** Ganges
알프스	산맥	**44.** Alps			황허 강	**68.** Huang
코카서스	산맥	**45.** Caucasus		**Rivers**	양자 강	**69.** Yangtze
우랄	산맥	**46.** Urals	강		적도	**70.** equator
히말라야	산맥	**47.** Himalayas	유콘강	**56.** Yukon	북쪽	**71.** north
			리오그랜데 강	**57.** Rio Grande	남쪽	**72.** south
	사막	**Deserts**	미시시피 강	**58.** Mississippi	동쪽	**73.** east
모자브	사막	**48.** Mojave	아마존 강	**59.** Amazon	서쪽	**74.** west
페인트스	사막	**49.** Painted	파라나 강	**60.** Paraná		
아타카마	사막	**50.** Atacama	니제르 강	**61.** Niger		
			콩고 강	**62.** Congo		

미합중국의 주명칭

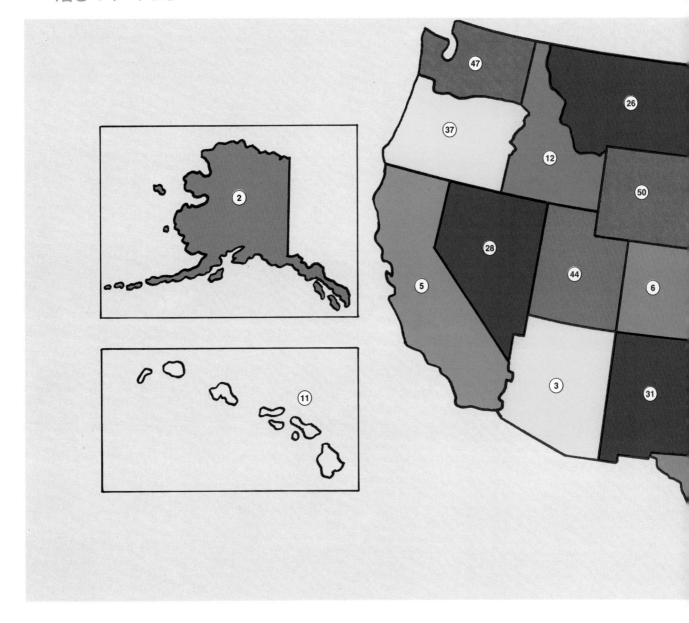

알라바마	**1.** Alabama		일리노이	**13.** Illinois
알라스카	**2.** Alaska		인디아나	**14.** Indiana
아리조나	**3.** Arizona		아이오아	**15.** Iowa
아칸사쓰	**4.** Arkansas		캔사스	**16.** Kansas
캘리포니아	**5.** California		켄터키	**17.** Kentucky
콜로라도	**6.** Colorado		루이지이아나	**18.** Louisiana
컨네티킽	**7.** Connecticut		메인	**19.** Maine
델라웨어	**8.** Delaware		매릴렌드	**20.** Maryland
플로리다	**9.** Florida		매사추세츠	**21.** Massachusetts
조오지아	**10.** Georgia		미시간	**22.** Michigan
화와이	**11.** Hawaii		미네쏘타	**23.** Minnesota
아이다호	**12.** Idaho		미시시피	**24.** Mississippi

미합중국의 주명칭

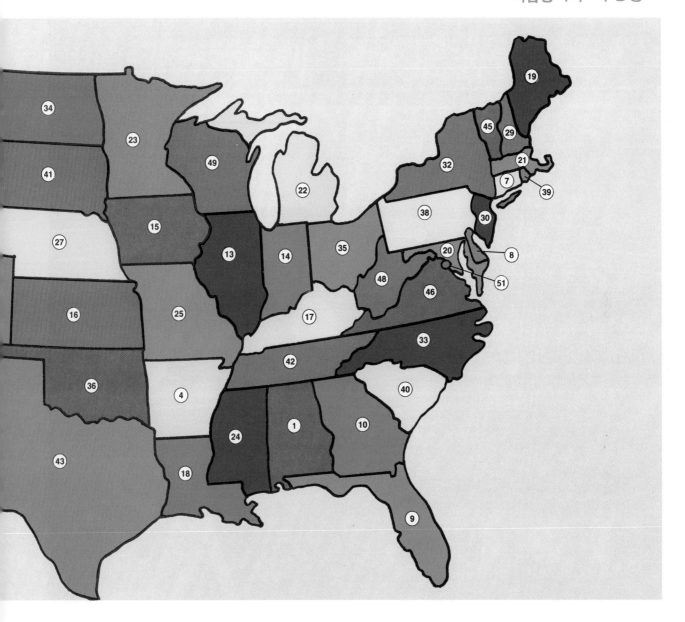

미조리	**25.** Missouri		로드아일랜드	**39.** Rhode Island
몬타나	**26.** Montana		싸우쓰캐롤리나	**40.** South Carolina
네브라스카	**27.** Nebraska		싸우쓰 다코타	**41.** South Dakota
네바다	**28.** Nevada		테네씨	**42.** Tennessee
뉴햄프셔	**29.** New Hampshire		텍사쓰	**43.** Texas
뉴저어지	**30.** New Jersey		유타	**44.** Utah
뉴맥시코	**31.** New Mexico		버몬트	**45.** Vermont
뉴욕	**32.** New York		버지니아	**46.** Virginia
노쓰캐롤리나	**33.** North Carolina		와싱톤	**47.** Washington
노쓰다코타	**34.** North Dakota		웨스트 버지니아	**48.** West Virginia
오하이오	**35.** Ohio		위스컨신	**49.** Wisconsin
오클라호마	**36.** Oklahoma		와이오밍	**50.** Wyoming
오레곤	**37.** Oregon			
펜실바니아	**38.** Pennsylvania		컬럼비아 특별지구	**51.** District of Columbia

대기권외	**A. Outer Space**		화성	**14.** Mars
은하수	**1.** galaxy		목성	**15.** Jupiter
혜성	**2.** comet		토성	**16.** Saturn
별자리	**3.** (Big Dipper) constellation		환	**a.** ring
별	**4.** star		천왕성	**17.** Uranus
유성	**5.** meteor		해왕성	**18.** Neptune
			명왕성	**19.** Pluto
태양계	**B. The Solar System**		소행성	**20.** asteroid
월식	**6.** lunar eclipse		궤도	**21.** orbit
태양	**7.** Sun		망원경	**22.** telescope
지구	**8.** Earth			
달	**9.** Moon		달의 위상	**C. Phases of the Moon**
일식	**10.** solar eclipse		상현	**23.** first quarter
			둥근달	**24.** full moon
행성	**The Planets**		하현	**25.** last quarter
수성	**11.** Mercury		초승달	**26.** new moon
금성	**12.** Venus			
지구	**13.** Earth			

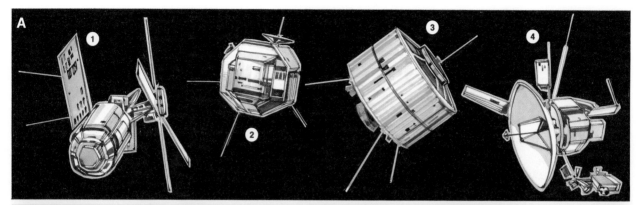

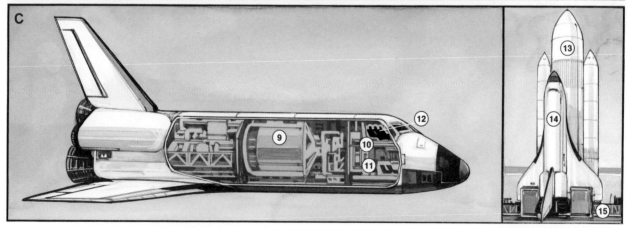

우주선	**A. Spacecraft**
우주 정류장	**1.** space station
통신 위성	**2.** communication satellite
기상 위성	**3.** weather satellite
우주 탐색기	**4.** space probe
달 착륙	**B. Landing on the Moon**
우주 비행사	**5.** astronaut
우주복	**6.** space suit
달 착륙선	**7.** lunar module
사령선	**8.** command module

우주 왕복선	**C. The Space Shuttle**
화물실	**9.** cargo bay
비행 갑판	**10.** flight deck
활동 구역	**11.** living quarters
승무원	**12.** crew
로케트	**13.** rocket
우주 왕복선	**14.** space shuttle
발사대	**15.** launchpad

교실

국기	**1.** flag		나선형 노트	**15.** spiral notebook
시계	**2.** clock		책상	**16.** desk
확성기	**3.** loudspeaker		풀	**17.** glue
교사	**4.** teacher		솔	**18.** brush
칠판	**5.** chalkboard		학생	**19.** student
휴대품 보관함	**6.** locker		연필깎이	**20.** pencil sharpener
게시판	**7.** bulletin board		연필 지우개	**21.** pencil eraser
콤퓨터	**8.** computer		볼펜	**22.** ballpoint pen
분필 받이	**9.** chalk tray		자	**23.** ruler
분필	**10.** chalk		연필	**24.** pencil
지우개	**11.** eraser		압핀	**25.** thumbtack
복도	**12.** hall		교과서	**26.** (text)book
루스리프식 종이	**13.** (loose-leaf) paper		오버헤드 프로젝터	**27.** overhead projector
철하는 표지	**14.** ring binder			

학교에서 쓰이는 동사

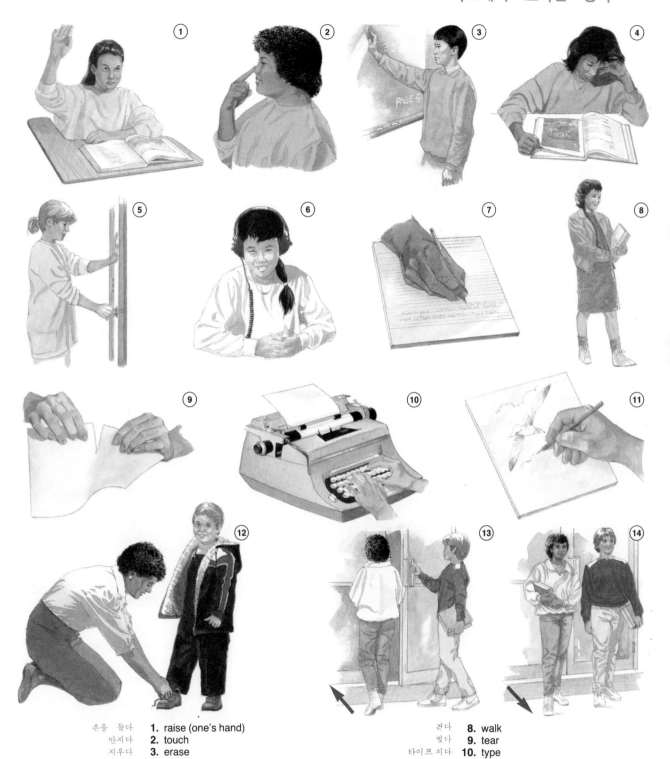

손을 들다	**1.** raise (one's hand)
만지다	**2.** touch
지우다	**3.** erase
읽다	**4.** read
닫다	**5.** close
듣다	**6.** listen
쓰다	**7.** write

걷다	**8.** walk
찢다	**9.** tear
타이프치다	**10.** type
그리다	**11.** draw
묶다	**12.** tie
떠나다	**13.** leave
들어가다	**14.** enter

과학   실험실

분광기	**1.** prism	고무관	**18.** rubber tubing
플래스크	**2.** flask	링스탠드	**19.** ring stand
박테리아 배양용 접시	**3.** petri dish	분젠 버너	**20.** Bunsen burner
저울	**4.** scale	불꽃	**21.** flame
무게추	**5.** weights	온도계	**22.** thermometer
철사로 짠 판	**6.** wire mesh screen	굽달린 큰 컵	**23.** beaker
죔쇠	**7.** clamp	진열대	**24.** bench
걸이	**8.** rack	눈금이 새겨진 유리 원 통	**25.** graduated cylinder
시험관	**9.** test tube	약 멸치개	**26.** medicine dropper
마개	**10.** stopper	자석	**27.** magnet
도표종이	**11.** graph paper	겸자 모양의 핀세트	**28.** forceps
안전용 유리안경	**12.** safety glasses	집게	**29.** tongs
멈춤용 시계	**13.** timer	현미경	**30.** microscope
가는 눈금있는 관	**14.** pipette	슬라이드	**31.** slide
확대경	**15.** magnifying glass	핀셋	**32.** tweezers
여과용 종이	**16.** filter paper	해부 기구	**33.** dissection kit
깔대기	**17.** funnel	등없는 걸상	**34.** stool

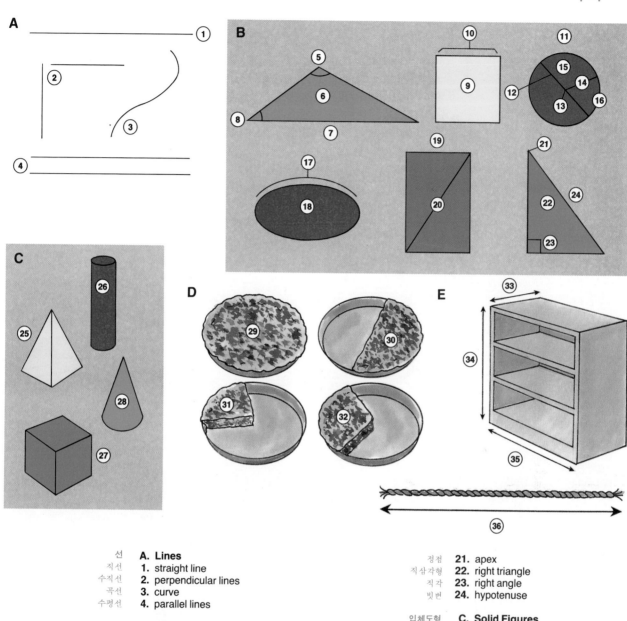

선   **A. Lines**
직선   **1.** straight line
수직선   **2.** perpendicular lines
곡선   **3.** curve
수평선   **4.** parallel lines

기하학적 도형 **B. Geometrical Figures**
둔각   **5.** obtuse angle
삼각형   **6.** triangle
밑변   **7.** base
예각   **8.** acute angle
정사각형   **9.** square
측면   **10.** side
원   **11.** circle
직경   **12.** diameter
중심부   **13.** center
반경   **14.** radius
절단면   **15.** section
호   **16.** arc
원주   **17.** circumference
타원형   **18.** oval
직사각형   **19.** rectangle
대각선   **20.** diagonal

정점   **21.** apex
직삼각형   **22.** right triangle
직각   **23.** right angle
빗변   **24.** hypotenuse

입체도형   **C. Solid Figures**
각뿔   **25.** pyramid
원기둥   **26.** cylinder
입방체   **27.** cube
원추체   **28.** cone

분수   **D. Fractions**
정수   **29.** whole
2분의 1   **30.** a half (1/2)
4분의 1   **31.** a quarter (1/4)
3분의 1   **32.** a third (1/3)

크기   **E. Measurement**
깊이   **33.** depth
높이   **34.** height
폭   **35.** width
길이   **36.** length

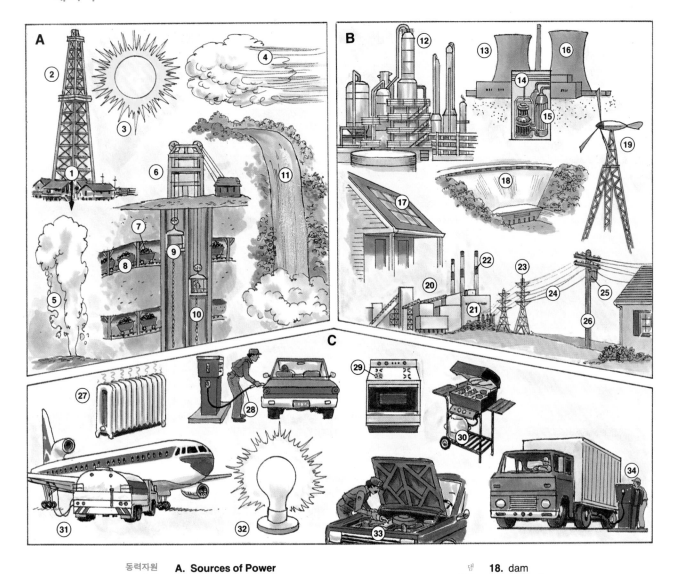

동력자원	**A. Sources of Power**
유정	**1.** oil well
유정탑	**2.** derrick
태양	**3.** sun
바람	**4.** wind
간헐천	**5.** geyser
탄광	**6.** coal mine
석탄	**7.** coal
간이차	**8.** shuttle car
승강기	**9.** elevator
수갱	**10.** shaft
폭포	**11.** waterfall

동력 생성장치	**B. Generation of Power**
정제소	**12.** refinery
원자로	**13.** nuclear reactor
원자로의 노심	**14.** core
우라늄 간	**15.** uranium rods
냉각탑	**16.** cooling tower
태양열 수집기	**17.** solar collector

댐	**18.** dam
풍차	**19.** windmill
발전소	**20.** power station
발전기	**21.** electrical generator
굴뚝	**22.** smokestack
전송탑	**23.** transmission towers
송전선	**24.** power lines
변압기	**25.** transformer
전신주	**26.** utility pole

용도 및 산물	**C. Uses and Products**
열	**27.** heat
휘발유	**28.** gas(oline)
천연가스	**29.** natural gas
프로판가스	**30.** propane gas
제트 연료	**31.** jet fuel
전기	**32.** electricity
자동차 기름	**33.** motor oil
디젤 연료	**34.** diesel fuel

낙농장	**A. Dairy Farm**	갈퀴	**14.** pitchfork
과수원	**1.** orchard	트랙터	**15.** tractor
과수	**2.** fruit tree	밀밭	**16.** (wheat) field
농장 안의 주택	**3.** farmhouse	베어내기및 탈곡용 농기계	**17.** combine
사일로	**4.** silo	줄	**18.** row
헛간	**5.** barn	허수아비	**19.** scarecrow
목장	**6.** pasture		
농부	**7.** farmer	방목장	**C. Ranch**
헛간의 앞마당	**8.** barnyard	가축	**20.** (herd of) cattle
울타리	**9.** fence	남자 목동	**21.** cowboy
양	**10.** sheep	여자 목동	**22.** cowgirl
젖소	**11.** dairy cow	말	**23.** horses
		가축 우리	**24.** corral
밀농장	**B. Wheat Farm**	구유(여물통)	**25.** trough
가축	**12.** livestock		
건초	**13.** (bale of) hay		

건축공사

건축 공사장	**A. Construction Site**		삽	15. shovel
서까래	1. rafters		판자	16. board
지붕널	2. shingle		보선공	17. linesman
수평기	3. level		인부용 이동 크레인	18. cherry picker
안전모	4. hard hat			
건축업자	5. builder		도로공사	**B. Road Work**
청사진	6. blueprints		원뿔꼴의 쇠뭉치	19. cone
작업 발판대	7. scaffolding		기	20. flag
사다리	8. ladder		통행 차단물	21. barricade
가로장	9. rung		소형 착암기	22. jackhammer
시멘트	10. cement		외바퀴 손수레	23. wheelbarrow
기초	11. foundation		중앙선 칸막이	24. center divider
벽돌	12. bricks		시멘트 배합기	25. cement mixer
곡괭이	13. pickax		흙걷어 치우는 기계	26. backhoe
전선 공사 인부	14. construction worker		불도저	27. bulldozer

사무실

교환수	**1.** switchboard operator
헤드폰	**2.** headset
교환대	**3.** switchboard
프린터	**4.** printer
칸막이한 작은방	**5.** cubicle
타자수	**6.** typist
자동 문서 작성기	**7.** word processor
프린트물	**8.** printout
달력	**9.** calendar
타자기	**10.** typewriter
비서	**11.** secretary
결재 서류함	**12.** in-box
책상	**13.** desk
참고철	**14.** rolodex
전화기	**15.** telephone
콤퓨터	**16.** computer

타자수용 의자	**17.** typing chair
지배인	**18.** manager
계산기	**19.** calculator
책꽂이	**20.** bookcase
서류 보관함	**21.** file cabinet
서류 끼우개	**22.** file folder
서류 정리원	**23.** file clerk
복사기	**24.** photocopier
전달 메모지	**25.** message pad
큰 종이철	**26.** (legal) pad
호치키스	**27.** stapler
종이 끼우개	**28.** paper clips
철쇠 제거기	**29.** staple remover
연필깎이	**30.** pencil sharpener
봉투	**31.** envelope

직업 (1) : 미국의 주된 업종

약사	**1.** pharmacist		빵류 제조 판매업자	**8.** baker
정비사	**2.** mechanic		안경상	**9.** optician
이발사	**3.** barber		미용사	**10.** hairdresser
여행 안내업자	**4.** travel agent		화초 재배자	**11.** florist
수선공	**5.** repairperson		보석상	**12.** jeweller
재단사	**6.** tailor		도살업자	**13.** butcher
야채 장수	**7.** greengrocer			

직업 (II)

수선 및 관리	**A. Repair and Maintenance**	가사와 관련된 업무	**B. Household Services**
배관공	**1.** plumber	파출부	**8.** housekeeper
목공	**2.** carpenter	청소부	**9.** janitor
정원사	**3.** gardener	배달원	**10.** delivery boy
자물쇠 제조장수	**4.** locksmith	수위	**11.** doorman
부동산업자	**5.** real estate agent		
전기 기술자	**6.** electrician	공장일	**C. Factory Work**
뺑끼장이	**7.** painter	공원	**12.** shop worker
		직공장	**13.** foreman

매스콤 및 기술	A. Media and Arts
관상대원	1. weather forecaster
뉴스 방송 해설자	2. newscaster
예술가	3. artist
사진사	4. photographer
모델	5. model
의상 연구가	6. fashion designer
작가	7. writer
건축가	8. architect
디스크 자키	9. disc jockey (DJ)
사진사	10. cameraperson
기자	11. reporter
판매원	12. salesperson

은행	B. Banking
은행 간부 직원	13. officer
경비원	14. security guard
은행원	15. teller

사무 종사자	C. Business Workers
콤퓨터 프로그램 작성자	16. computer programmer
접수계원	17. receptionist
회계사	18. accountant
심부름꾼	19. messenger

동물원	**1.** zoo
야외 음악당	**2.** band shell
행상인	**3.** vendor
손수레	**4.** hand truck
회전 목마	**5.** merry-go-round
말타는 사람	**6.** horseback rider
승마 길	**7.** bridle path
연못	**8.** (duck) pond
조깅길	**9.** jogging path
긴의자	**10.** bench

쓰레기통	**11.** trash can
미끄럼틀	**12.** slide
모래놀이통	**13.** sandbox
물뿌리개	**14.** sprinkler
놀이터	**15.** playground
그네	**16.** swings
철골·나무로 된 운동시설	**17.** jungle gym
시소놀이	**18.** seesaw
분수식의 물 마시는 곳	**19.** water fountain

야영　활동

고원	**1.** plateau	소풍 지역	**Picnic Area**
도보 여행자	**2.** hikers	석쇠	**12.** grill
협곡	**3.** canyon	소풍 바구리	**13.** picnic basket
언덕	**4.** hill	보온병	**14.** thermos
공원 순찰대	**5.** park ranger	소풍용 간이 식탁	**15.** picnic table
낚시질	**Fishing**		
개울	**6.** stream		
낚싯대	**7.** fishing rod		
낚싯줄	**8.** fishing line		
그물	**9.** fishing net		
방수복	**10.** waders		
바위	**11.** rocks		

고무 보우트 놀이	**Rafting**		야영	**Camping**
고무 보우트	**16.** raft		천막	**24.** tent
급류	**17.** rapids		야영용 스토브	**25.** camp stove
폭포	**18.** waterfall		침낭	**26.** sleeping bag
			멜빵고리	**27.** gear
등산	**Mountain Climbing**		등짐 기구	**28.** frame backpack
산	**19.** mountain		랜턴	**29.** lantern
산꼭대기	**20.** peak		말뚝	**30.** stake
절벽	**21.** cliff		모닥불	**31.** campfire
등산용 멜빵	**22.** harness		숲	**32.** woods
줄	**23.** rope			

<table>
<tr><td>해변의 널을 깐 보도</td><td>**1.** boardwalk</td><td>모래 언덕</td><td>**12.** sand dunes</td></tr>
<tr><td>간이 음식점</td><td>**2.** refreshment stand</td><td>프리스비</td><td>**13.** Frisbee ™</td></tr>
<tr><td>자동차 여행자 숙박소</td><td>**3.** motel</td><td>색안경</td><td>**14.** sunglasses</td></tr>
<tr><td>자전거를 타는 사람</td><td>**4.** biker</td><td>해변에 까는 수건</td><td>**15.** beach towel</td></tr>
<tr><td>호각</td><td>**5.** whistle</td><td>바께쓰</td><td>**16.** pail</td></tr>
<tr><td>구조원</td><td>**6.** lifeguard</td><td>모래삽</td><td>**17.** shovel</td></tr>
<tr><td>쌍안경</td><td>**7.** binoculars</td><td>수영복</td><td>**18.** bathing suit</td></tr>
<tr><td>구조원용 의자</td><td>**8.** lifeguard chair</td><td>일광욕하는 사람</td><td>**19.** sunbather</td></tr>
<tr><td>구명구</td><td>**9.** life preserver</td><td>해변용 긴 의자</td><td>**20.** beach chair</td></tr>
<tr><td>구명정</td><td>**10.** lifeboat</td><td>비치 파라솔</td><td>**21.** beach umbrella</td></tr>
<tr><td>해변용 큰 공</td><td>**11.** beach ball</td><td></td><td></td></tr>
</table>

연	**22.** kite	모래성	**32.** sandcastle
달리는 사람	**23.** runners	남성용 수영팬츠	**33.** bathing trunks
파도	**24.** wave	잠수중에 호흡하는 관	**34.** snorkel
파도 타기용 널	**25.** surfboard	수중 마스크	**35.** mask
압축용 매트레스	**26.** air mattress	잠수용 고무 발갈퀴	**36.** flippers
킥보드(잡고 타는 판자)	**27.** kickboard	잠수용 산소 탱크	**37.** scuba tank
수영하는 사람	**28.** swimmer	잠수용의 고무옷	**38.** wet suit
둥근 고무관	**29.** tube	그을름 방지용 세제	**39.** suntan lotion
바닷물	**30.** water	조개 껍질	**40.** shell
모래	**31.** sand	휴대용 아이스박스	**41.** cooler

단체 운동 경기

야구	**Baseball**
심판관	**1.** umpire
포수	**2.** catcher
포수용 얼굴 가리개	**3.** catcher's mask
포수용 미트	**4.** catcher's mitt
야구 방망이	**5.** bat
타자용 안전모	**6.** batting helmet
타자	**7.** batter

어린이 야구	**Little League Baseball**
어린이 야구선수	**8.** Little Leaguer
유니폼	**9.** uniform

소프트 볼	**Softball**
소프트 볼 공	**10.** softball
모자	**11.** cap
야구용 글러브	**12.** glove

미식 축구	**Football**
미식 축구공	**13.** football
미식 축구용 안전모	**14.** helmet

라크로스 (하키 비슷한 구기의 일종)	**Lacrosse**
얼굴 가리개	**15.** face guard
라크로스 스틱	**16.** lacrosse stick

아이스하키	**Ice Hockey**
아이스하키용 퍽	**17.** puck
하키용 스틱	**18.** hockey stick

농구	**Basketball**
백보드	**19.** backboard
골그물	**20.** basket
농구공	**21.** basketball

배구	**Volleyball**
배구공	**22.** volleyball
네트	**23.** net

축구	**Soccer**
문지기	**24.** goalie
골문	**25.** goal
축구공	**26.** soccer ball

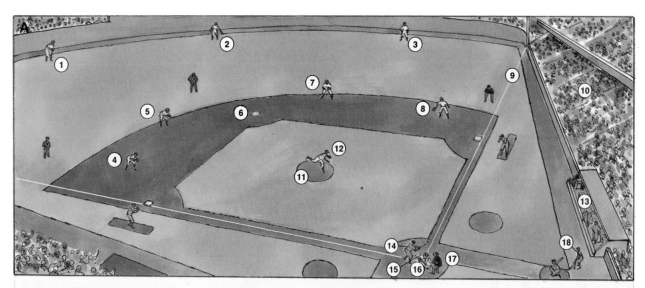

야구장	**A. Baseball Diamond**	미식 축구장	**B. Football Field**
좌익수	1. left fielder	득점판	19. scoreboard
중견수	2. center fielder	응원단장	20. cheerleaders
우익수	3. right fielder	코치	21. coach
3루수	4. third baseman	심판관	22. referee
유격수	5. shortstop	전위 양끝의 선	23. end zone
누 (베이스)	6. base	스플릿 엔드 (공격측의 끝)	24. split end
2루수	7. second baseman	엔드와 가드 사이의 좌측전위	25. left tackle
1루수	8. first baseman	좌측 가드	26. left guard
파울라인	9. foul line	센터	27. center
관람석	10. stands	우측 가드	28. right guard
투수가 서는 마운드	11. pitcher's mound	우측 전위	29. right tackle
투수	12. pitcher	공격 끝선	30. tight end
선수 대기소	13. dugout	측면 공격수	31. flanker
타자	14. batter	쿼터백	32. quarterback
본루	15. home plate	중위	33. halfback
포수	16. catcher	후위	34. fullback
심판관	17. umpire	골대	35. goalpost
야구팀의 잡일을 보는 소년	18. batboy		

개인 스포츠

테니스	**Tennis**
테니스 공	**1.** tennis ball
라케트	**2.** racket
볼링	**Bowling**
레인 양쪽의 홈	**3.** gutter
레인	**4.** lane
볼링 표주	**5.** pin
볼링 공	**6.** bowling ball
골프	**Golf**
골프 공	**7.** golf ball
구멍	**8.** hole
골프 채	**9.** putter
골프치는 사람	**10.** golfer
핸드볼 (송구)	**Handball**
글러브	**11.** glove
핸드볼 공	**12.** handball
코트	**13.** court
권투	**Boxing**
머리 보호장치	**14.** head protector
글러브	**15.** glove
심판관	**16.** referee
권투장	**17.** ring
탁구	**Ping-Pong**
라케트	**18.** paddle
탁구공	**19.** ping-pong ball

말타기	**Horse Racing**
안장	**20.** saddle
경마의 기수	**21.** jockey
고삐	**22.** reins
체조	**Gymnastics**
체조사	**23.** gymnast
평균대	**24.** balance beam
빙상 스케이트	**Ice Skating**
스케이트장	**25.** rink
스케이트	**26.** skate
스케이트 날	**27.** blade
라케트 경기	**Racquetball**
보호 안경	**28.** safety goggles
라케트	**29.** racquet
라케트 공	**30.** racquetball
육상 경기	**Track and Field**
주자	**31.** runner
경주로	**32.** track
전원 스키	**Cross-Country Skiing**
스키	**33.** skis
스킷대	**34.** pole
스키타는 사람	**35.** skier

필 드 및 코 스 경 기

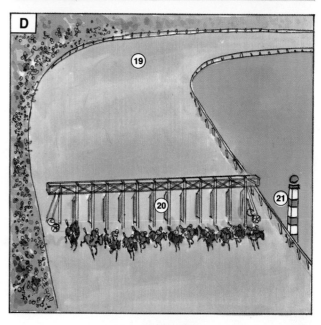

테니스 장	**A. Tennis Court**
서브를 넣는 코트	**1.** service court
네트	**2.** net
서브 라인	**3.** service line
코트의 끝선	**4.** baseline
골프 코스	**B. Golf Course**
골프채	**5.** clubs
골프장밖의 잡조가 우거진 곳	**6.** rough
골프백	**7.** golf bag
골프 카트	**8.** golf cart
기	**9.** flag
골프 코스	**10.** green
모래 구덩이	**11.** sand trap
구좌와 그린 사이의 잔디구역	**12.** fairway
구좌(공 울려 놓는 자리)	**13.** tee

스키장	**C. Ski Slope**
버팀대	**14.** pole
스키화	**15.** ski boot
스키화 죄는 기구	**16.** binding
스키	**17.** ski
스키 리프트	**18.** ski lift
경마장	**D. Race Track**
직선 코스	**19.** stretch
출발점	**20.** starting gate
결승선	**21.** finish line·

운동에 관한 동사

치다	**1.** hit	보내다	**5.** pass
서브하다	**2.** serve	달리다	**6.** run
차다	**3.** kick	넘어지다	**7.** fall
잡다	**4.** catch	뛰다	**8.** jump

스케이트를 타다	**9.** skate
던지다	**10.** throw
튀기다	**11.** bounce
파도를 타다	**12.** surf

타다(자전거 · 말등)	**13.** ride
다이브하다	**14.** dive
운전하다	**15.** drive
쏘다	**16.** shoot

악기

현악기	**Strings**
피아노	**1.** piano
건반	**a.** keyboard
한장의 악보로 인쇄된 팝뮤직	**2.** sheet music
네줄 소형 기타	**3.** ukulele
만도린	**4.** mandolin
밴조	**5.** banjo
하프	**6.** harp
바이올린	**7.** violin
활.	**a.** bow
비올라	**8.** viola
첼로	**9.** cello
바스	**10.** bass
현	**a.** string
기타	**11.** guitar
픽	**a.** pick

목관악기	**Woodwinds**
피콜로	**12.** piccolo
피리	**13.** flute
저음의 목관악기	**14.** bassoon
오보에	**15.** oboe
클리리넷	**16.** clarinet

타악기	**Percussion**
방울달린 작은 북	**17.** tambourine
심벌즈	**18.** cymbals
북	**19.** drum
북채	**a.** drumsticks
콩카 드럼	**20.** conga
솥 모양의 큰북	**21.** kettledrum
작은북	**22.** bongos

금관악기	**Brass**
저음의 큰 나팔	**23.** trombone
색스폰	**24.** saxophone
트럼펫	**25.** trumpet
프렌치혼	**26.** French horn
튜바	**27.** tuba

기타 악기류	**Other Instruments**
아코디언	**28.** accordion
오르간	**29.** organ
하모니카	**30.** harmonica
실로폰	**31.** xylophone

발레	**A. The Ballet**	
커튼	**1.** curtain	
무대장면	**2.** scenery	
무용수	**3.** dancer	
조명	**4.** spotlight	
무대	**5.** stage	
관현악단	**6.** orchestra	
지휘대	**7.** podium	
지휘자	**8.** conductor	
지휘봉	**9.** baton	
음악가	**10.** musician	
박스석	**11.** box seat	
주악석	**12.** orchestra seating	
중이층	**13.** mezzanine	
발코니	**14.** balcony	
청중	**15.** audience	
안내인	**16.** usher	
프로그램	**17.** programs	

회가극	**B. Musical Comedy**	
합창단	**18.** chorus	
남배우	**19.** actor	
여배우	**20.** actress	

록그룹	**C. Rock Group**	
전자음향 합성장치	**21.** synthesizer	
전반악기 연주자	**22.** keyboard player	
저음 기타수	**23.** bass guitarist	
가수	**24.** singer	
기타 단장	**25.** lead guitarist	
전자 기타	**26.** electric guitar	
북 연주자	**27.** drummer	

전자제품 및 사진술

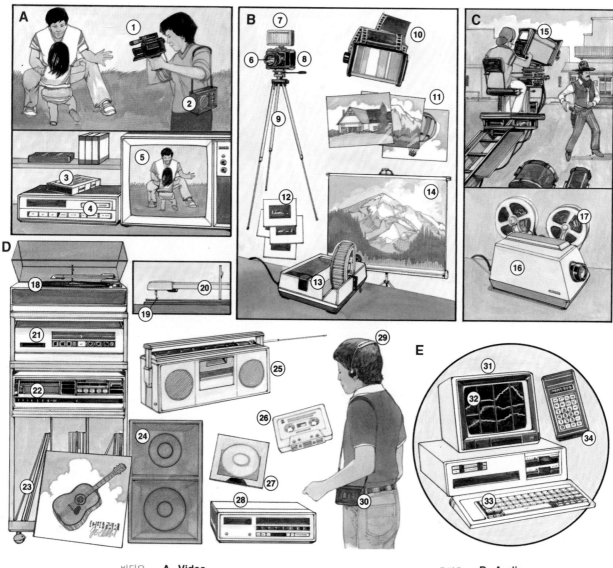

비디오	**A. Video**
비디오 카메라	**1.** video camera
소형 카메라	**2.** Minicam ™
비디오테이프	**3.** videocassette (tape)
비디오 녹화기	**4.** VCR (videocassette recorder)
텔레비전	**5.** television
사진술	**B. Photography**
렌즈	**6.** lens
플래시	**7.** flash
사진기	**8.** camera
삼각대	**9.** tripod
필름	**10.** (roll of) film
인화된 사진	**11.** prints
슬라이드	**12.** slides
슬라이드 장치기계	**13.** slide projector
스크린	**14.** screen
필름	**C. Film**
영화 촬영기	**15.** movie camera
영사기	**16.** projector
필름	**17.** (reel of) film

오디오	**D. Audio**
회전판	**18.** turntable
전축 바늘	**19.** cartridge needle
팔	**20.** arm
수신기	**21.** receiver
카세트 덱	**22.** cassette deck
레코드	**23.** records
스피커	**24.** speaker
스테레오 카세트 플레이어	**25.** stereo cassette player
카세트	**26.** cassette
콤팩트 디스크	**27.** compact disc (CD)
콤팩트 디스크 플레이어	**28.** compact disc player
헤드폰	**29.** headphones
쏘니 휴대용 카세트 플레이어	**30.** Sony Walkman
콤퓨터	**E. Computers**
개인용 콤퓨터	**31.** personal computer (PC)
모니터	**32.** monitor
키보드	**33.** keyboard
전자 계산기	**34.** calculator

재봉	**A. Sewing**		가위	**17.** (pair of) scissors
재봉틀	**1.** sewing machine		바늘	**18.** needle
실패	**2.** (spool of) thread		바늘뜸	**19.** stitch
바늘꽂이	**3.** pincushion		핀	**20.** pin
양복의 감	**4.** material		골무	**21.** thimble
핑킹용 가위	**5.** pinking shears			
견본	**6.** pattern piece		기타 수공예	**B. Other Needlecrafts**
도안	**7.** pattern		뜨개질	**22.** knitting
단추구멍	**8.** buttonhole		털실	**23.** wool
단추	**9.** button		실타래	**24.** skein
솔기	**10.** seam		뜨개바늘	**25.** knitting needle
헴	**11.** hem		바늘 끝	**26.** needlepoint
헴칩	**12.** hem binding		자수	**27.** embroidery
눌림쇠	**13.** snap		코바늘 뜨개질	**28.** crochet
갈고리 및 눈	**14.** hook and eye		코바늘	**29.** crochet hook
줄자	**15.** tape measure		짜는 행위	**30.** weaving
지퍼	**16.** zipper		털실	**31.** yarn
			누빔	**32.** quilting

위치에 관한 전치사

(창문가) 에 (서)	**1.** at (the window)
(검은고양이) 위에 (서)	**2.** above (the black cat)
(하얀 고양이) 아래에 (서)	**3.** below (the white cat)
(벼개) 사이에 (서)	**4.** between (the pillows)
(양탄자) 위에 (서)	**5.** on (the rug)
(화닥) 앞에 (서)	**6.** in front of (the fireplace)

(서랍) 안에 (서)	**7.** in (the drawer)
(책상) 밑에 (서)	**8.** under (the desk)
(의자) 뒤에 (서)	**9.** behind (the chair)
(식탁) 위에 (서)	**10.** on top of (the table)
(테레비) 옆에 (서)	**11.** next to (the TV)

(등대를) 통하여 (서)	**1.** through (the lighthouse)	(물) 밖으로	**7.** out of (the water)
(등대) 근처에 (서)	**2.** around (the lighthouse)	(다리) 위로	**8.** over (the bridge)
(언덕) 밑에 (서)	**3.** down (the hill)	(골프장) 쪽으로	**9.** to (the course)
(구멍을) 향하여	**4.** toward (the hole)	(골프장) 에서, 으로부터	**10.** from (the course)
(구멍) 에서 멀리	**5.** away from (the hole)	(언덕) 위로	**11.** up (the hill)
(물을) 건너서	**6.** across (the water)	(구멍) 속으로	**12.** into (the hole)

부록

주의 요일	**Days of the Week**
일요일	Sunday
월요일	Monday
화요일	Tuesday
수요일	Wednesday
목요일	Thursday
금요일	Friday
토요일	Saturday

연 월	**Months of the Year**
일월	January
이월	February
삼월	March
사월	April
오월	May
유월	June
칠월	July
팔월	August
구월	September
시월	October
십일월	November
십이월	December

수	**Numbers**	
영	0	zero
하나(일)	1	one
둘(이)	2	two
셋(삼)	3	three
넷(사)	4	four
다섯(오)	5	five
여섯(육)	6	six
일곱(칠)	7	seven
여덟(팔)	8	eight
아홉(구)	9	nine
열(십)	10	ten
열하나(십일)	11	eleven
열둘(십이)	12	twelve
열셋(십삼)	13	thirteen
열넷(십사)	14	fourteen
열다섯(십오)	15	fifteen
열여섯(십육)	16	sixteen
열일곱(십칠)	17	seventeen
열여덟(십팔)	18	eighteen
열아홉(십구)	19	nineteen
스물(이십)	20	twenty
스물하나(이십일)	21	twenty-one
설혼(삼십)	30	thirty
마흔(사십)	40	forty
쉬흔(오십)	50	fifty
예순(육십)	60	sixty
일흔(칠십)	70	seventy
여든(팔십)	80	eighty
아흔(구십)	90	ninety
백	100	a/one hundred
오백	500	five hundred
육백이십일	621	six hundred (and) twenty-one
(일)천	1,000	a/one thousand
(일)백만	1,000,000	a/one million

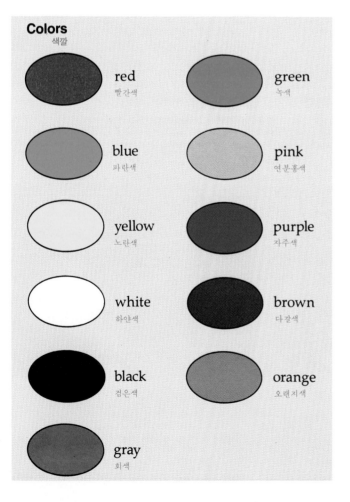

Colors
색깔

red
빨간색

green
녹색

blue
파란색

pink
연분홍색

yellow
노란색

purple
자주색

white
하얀색

brown
다갈색

black
검은색

orange
오래지색

gray
회색

Two numbers occur after words in the index: the first refers to the page where the word is illustrated and the second to the item number of the word on that page. For example, above [ə bŭv⁄] **102** 2 means that the word *above* is the item numbered 2 on page 102. If only a bold number appears, then that word is part of the unit title or a subtitle.

The index includes a pronunciation guide for all the words illustrated in the book. This guide uses symbols commonly found in dictionaries for native speakers. These symbols, unlike those used in transcription systems such as the International Phonetic Alphabet, tend to preserve spelling and so should help you to become more aware of the connections between written English and spoken English.

Consonants

[b] as in **back** [băk]   [k] as in **kite** [kīt]   [sh] as in **shell** [shĕl]
[ch] as in **cheek** [chēk]   [l] as in **leaf** [lēf]   [t] as in **tape** [tāp]
[d] as in **date** [dāt]   [m] as in **man** [măn]   [th] as in **three** [thrē]
[dh] as in **the** [dh]   [n] as in **neck** [nĕk]   [v] as in **vine** [vīn]
[f] as in **face** [fās]   [ng] as in **ring** [rĭng]   [w] as in **waist** [wāst]
[g] as in **gas** [găs]   [p] as in **pack** [păk]   [y] as in **yam** [yăm]
[h] as in **half** [hăf]   [r] as in **rake** [rāk]   [z] as in **zoo** [zōō]
[j] as in **jack** [jăk]   [s] as in **sand** [sănd]   [zh] as in **measure** [mĕzh⁄ər]

Vowels

[ā] as in **bake** [bāk]   [ī] as in **lime** [līm]   [ōō] as in **cool** [kōōl]
[ă] as in **back** [băk]   [ĭ] as in **lip** [lĭp]   [ŏŏ] as in **book** [bŏŏk]
[ä] as in **bar** [bär]   [ï] as in **beer** [bïr]   [ow] as in **cow** [kow]
[ē] as in **beat** [bēt]   [ō] as in **post** [pōst]   [oy] as in **boy** [boy]
[ĕ] as in **bed** [bĕd]   [ŏ] as in **box** [bŏks]   [ŭ] as in **cut** [kŭt]
[ë] as in **bear** [bër]   [ö] as in **claw** [klö]   [ü] as in **curb** [kürb]
                               or **for** [för]   [ə] as in **above** [ə bŭv⁄]

All pronunciation symbols used are alphabetical except for the schwa [ə], which is the most frequent vowel sound in English. If you use it appropriately in unstressed syllables, your pronunciation will sound more natural.

You should note that an umlaut ([¨]) calls attention to the special quality of vowels before [r]. (The sound [ö] can also represent a vowel not followed by [r] as in *claw.*) You should listen carefully to native speakers to discover how these vowels actually sound.

Stress

This guide also follows the system for marking stress used in many dictionaries for native speakers.
   (1) Stress is not marked if a word consisting of a single syllable occurs in isolation.
   (2) Where stress is marked, two levels are distinguished:
      a bold accent [⁄] is placed after each syllable with primary stress,
      a light accent [⁄] is placed after each syllable with secondary stress.

Syllable Boundaries

Syllable boundaries are indicated by a single space.

NOTE: The pronunciation used in this index is based on patterns of American English. There has been no attempt to represent all of the varieties of American English. Students should listen to native speakers to hear how the language actually sounds in a particular region.

above [ə bŭv′] **102** 2

abdomen [ăb′də mən] **4** 14

accelerator [ăk sĕl′ə rā′tər] **50** 27

accordian [ə kör′dē ən] **98** 28

accountant [ə kown′tənt] **86** 18

acorn [ā′körn] **60** 33c

acorn squash [ā′körn skwŏsh′] **6** 28

across [ə krös′] **103** 6

actor [ăk′tər] **99** 19

actress [ăk′trəs] **99** 20

acute angle [ə kyo͞ot′ ăng′gəl] **79** 8

address [ă′drĕs] **46** 11

adjectives [ăj′ĭk tĭvz] **24, 25**

aerial tramway [ĕr′ē əl trăm′wā] **54** 3

Africa [ă′frĭ kə] **70** 4

after-shave lotion [ăf′tər shāv lō′shən] **23** 2

ailments [āl′mənts] **40**

air conditioner [ĕr′ kən dĭ′shə nər] **32** 11

air filter [ĕr′ fĭl′tər] **50** 52

Air Force [ĕr′ förs′] **48** 19

air mattress [ĕr′ mă′trəs] **90** 26

air pump [ĕr′ pŭmp′] **53** 13

air travel [ĕr′ tră′vəl] **56**

aircraft [ĕr′krăft′] **57**

aircraft carrier [ĕr′krăft kăr′yər] **48** 4

aircraft types [ĕr′krăft tīps′] **57**

(airmail) envelope [ĕr′māl ĕn′və lōp] **46** 16

airman [ĕr′mən] **48** 20

airport check-in [ĕr′pört chĕk′ĭn] **56**

aisle [ī′əl] **14** 10, **56** 23

Alabama [ăl′ə bă′mə] **72** 1

alarm clock [ə lärm′ klŏk′] **32** 8

Alaska [ə lăs′kə] **72** 2

alcohol [ăl′kə höl′] **39** 22

alligator [ăl′ə gā′tər] **65** 8

almond(s) [ö′mənd(z)] **8** 31

Alps [ălps] **70** 44

Amazon River [ă′mə zŏn rĭv′ər] **70** 59

ambulance [ăm′byə ləns] **42** 6

amphibians [ăm fĭ′bē ənz] **65**

ammunition [ăm′yə nĭsh′ən] **48**

anchor [ăng′kər] **58** 24

Andes [ăn′dēz] **70** 43

ankle [ăng′kəl] **4** 49

animals [ăn′ə məlz] **62-69**

ant [ănt] **63** 12

Antarctic Ocean [ănt ärk′tĭk ō′shən] **70** 14

Antarctica [ănt ärk′tĭ kə] **70** 7

anteater [ănt′ē′tər] **66** 5

antenna [ăn tĕn′ə] **50** 46, **62** 1b

antler [ănt′lər] **66** 35a

apartment house [ə pärt′mənt hows′] **44** 23

apex [ā′pĕks] **79** 21

Appalachian Mountains [ăp′ə lā′chē ən mown′tənz] **70** 41

apple [ă′pəl] **8** 2

apricot [ăp′rə kŏt′] **8** 25

apron [ā′prən] **16** 6

aquatic mammals [ə kwŏ′tĭk mă′məlz] **68**

Arabian Sea [ə rā′bē ən sē′] **70** 30

arc [ärk] **79** 16

architect [är′kə tĕkt′] **86** 8

Arctic [ärk′tĭk] **70** 8

Arizona [ăr′ə zō′nə] **72** 3

Arkansas [är′kən sö′] **72** 4

arm [ärm] **4** 6, **100** 20

armadillo [är′mə dĭl′ō] **66** 2

armed forces [ärmd′ för′səz] **48**

armpit [ärm′pĭt′] **4** 10

armrest [ärm′rĕst′] **50** 3

Army [är′mē] **48** 15

around [ə rownd′] **103** 2

artery [är′tə rē] **4** 69

artichoke [är′tə chōk′] **6** 11

artist [är′təst] **86** 3

arts [ärts] **86**

ashtray [ăsh′trā′] **16** 29

Asia [ā′zhə] **70** 5

asparagus [ə spăr′ə gəs] **6** 18

asteroid [ăs′tə royd′] **74** 20

astronaut [ăs′trə nŏt′] **75** 5

at [ăt] **102** 1

Atacama Desert [ăt′ə kŏ′mə dĕz′ərt] **70** 50

athletic supporter [ăth lĕ′tĭk sə pör′tər] **22** 4

atlas [ăt′ləs] **47** 20

attachments [ə tăch′mənts] **35** 17

attendant [ə tĕn′dənt] **39** 8, **53** 12

audience [ö′dē əns] **99** 15

audio [ö′dē ō′] **100**

aunt [ănt] **3** 6

Australia [ö strāl′yə] **70** 6

author [ö′thər] **47** 8

automatic transmission [ö′tə măt′ĭk trănz mĭ′shən] **50**

avocado [ăv′ə kŏ′dō] **8** 33

away from [ə wā′ frŭm] **103** 5

axe [ăks] **42** 14

baboon [bă bo͞on′] **68** 19

baby [bā′bē] **2** 5

baby carriage [bā′bē kăr′ĭj] **44** 27

baby lotion [bā′bē lō′shən] **33** 6

baby powder [bā′bē pow′dər] **33** 7

baby wipes [bā′bē wīps′] **33** 8

baby's room [bā′bēz ro͞om′] **33**

back [băk] **4** 11, **23** 19

backache [băk′āk′] **40** 8

backboard [băk′börd′] **92** 19

backhoe [băk′hō′] **82** 26

backpack [băk′păk′] **19** 4

backseat [băk′sēt′] **50** 32

backyard [băk′yärd′] **27**

back-up light [băk′əp līt′] **50** 30

bacon [bā′kən] **10** 11, **18** 33

badge [băj] **43** 5

Baffin Bay [băf′ən bā′] **70** 16

bag [băg] **12** 8, **14** 25, **20** 35

baggage [băg′ĭj] **56** 8

bake [bāk] **31** 14

baked beans [bākt′ bēnz′] **18** 3

baked goods [bākt′ go͝odz′] **14** 11

baked potato [bākt′ pə tā′tō] **18** 20

baker [bā′kər] **84** 8

bakery [bā′kə rē] **44** 6

balance beam [băl′əns bēm′] **94** 24

balcony [băl′kə nē] **99** 14

(bale of) hay [bāl′ əv hā′] **81** 13

ball [böl] **4** 52

ballet [bă lā′] **99**

ballfields [böl′fēldz′] **93**

ballpoint pen [böl′poynt pĕn′] **76** 22

Baltic Sea [böl′tĭk sē′] **70** 22

bananas [bə nă′nəz] **8** 20

Band-Aid [băndʹād′] **39** 4

band shell [bănd′ shĕl′] **87** 2

bandage [băn′dĭj] **39** 24

banister [băn′ə stər] **28** 11

banjo [băn′jō′] **98** 5

banking [băng′kĭng] **86**

bar [bär] **12** 18, **16** 24

bar stool [bär′sto͞ol′] **16** 25

barber [bär′bər] **84** 3

Barents Sea [băr′ənts sē′] **70** 23

barge [bärj] **58** 12

bark [bärk] **60** 35c

barn [bärn] **81** 5

barnyard [bärn′yärd′] **81** 8

barrel [băr′əl] **48** 23

barricade [băr′ə kād′] **82** 21

bartender [bär′tĕn′dər] **16** 21

base [bās] **79** 7, **93** 6

baseball [bās′böl′] **92**

baseball diamond [bās′böl dī′mənd] **93**

baseline [bās′līn′] **95** 4

basin [bā′sən] **39** 16

basket [băs′kət] **92** 20

basketball [băs′kət böl′] **92, 92** 21

bass [bās] **98** 10

bass guitarist [bās′gə tär′əst] **99** 23

bassoon [bă soon′] **98** 14

bat [băt] **66** 4, **92** 5

batboy [băt′boy′] **93** 18

bath mat [băth′ măt′] **34** 12

bath towel [băth′ tow′əl] **34** 24

bathing suit [bā′dhĭng soot′] **90** 18

bathing trunks [bā′dhĭng trŭngks′] **90** 33

bathrobe [băth′rōb′] **22** 20

bathroom [băth′room′] **34**

bathtub [băth′tŭb′] **34** 11

baton [bə tŏn′] **99** 9

batter [băt′ər] **92** 7, **93** 14

battery [băt′ə rē] **50** 54

batting helmet [băt′ĭng hĕl′mət] **92** 6

battleship [băt′əl shĭp′] **48** 5

Bay of Bengal [bā′ əv bĕn göl′] **70** 32

bayonet [bā′ə nĕt′] **48** 24

bays [bāz] **70**

beach [bēch] **90**

beach ball [bēch′ böl′] **90** 11

beach chair [bēch′ chër′] **90** 20

beach towel [bēch′ tow′əl] **90** 15

beach umbrella [bēch′ əm brĕl′ə] **90** 21

beads [bēdz] **23** 7

beak [bēk] **64** 3a

beaker [bē′kər] **78** 23

beard [bïrd] **4** 39

bears [bërz] **68**

beat [bēt] **31** 8

Beaufort Sea [bō′fərt sē′] **70** 15

beaver [bē′vər] **66** 12

bed [bĕd] **32** 21

bed rest [bĕd′ rĕst′] **41** 1

bedroom [bĕd′room′] **32**

bedspread [bĕd′sprĕd′] **32** 23

bee [bē] **63** 19

beef [bēf] **10** 1

beef stew [bēf′ stoo′] **18** 14

beer [bïr] **16** 23

beet(s) [bēts] **6** 33

beetle [bē′təl] **63** 10

behind [bə hīnd′] **102** 9

below [bə lō′] **102** 3

belt [bĕlt] **20** 16

bench [bĕnch] **43** 16, **44** 14, **78** 24, **87** 10

beret [bə rā′] **19** 22

Bering Sea [bër′ĭng sē′] **70** 34

berries [bër′ēz] **8**

between [bə twēn′] **102** 3

beverages [bĕv′rə jəz] **14** 14

bib [bĭb] **33** 20

bicycle [bī′sĭ kəl] **52** 15

big [bĭg] **24** 8

(Big Dipper) constellation [bĭg′ dĭ′pər kŏn stə lā′shən] **74** 3

big toe [bĭg′ tō′] **4** 53

bike stand [bīk′ stănd′] **52** 14

biker [bī′kər] **90** 4

bikes [bīks] **52**

(bikini) panties [bə kē′nē păn′tēz] **22** 11

bill [bĭl] **64** 24a

bin [bĭn] **14** 16

binding [bīn′dĭng] **95** 16

binoculars [bə nŏk′yə lərs] **90** 7

birch [bürch] **60** 32

birds [bürdz] **64**

biscuit [bĭs′kət] **18** 27

bison [bī′sən] **66** 19

bit [bĭt] **36** 43a

black bear [blăk′ bër′] **68** 21

black bean(s) [blăk′ bēn(z)′] **6** 14

black eye [blăk′ ī′] **40** 5

Black Sea [blăk′ sē′] **70** 26

blackberries [blăk′bër′ēz] **8** 12

bladder [blă′dər] **4** 72

blade [blād] **94** 27

blanket [blăng′kət] **32** 20

blazer [blā′zər] **20** 2

bleach [blēch] **35** 26

blender [blĕn′dər] **30** 12

blimp [blĭmp] **57** 5

blinds [blīndz] **32** 12

block [blŏk] **33** 32

blouse [blows] **20** 34

blue jay [bloo′ jā′] **64** 8

(blue) jeans [bloo′ jēnz′] **19** 6

blueberries [bloo′bër′ēz] **8** 14

blue prints [bloo′ prĭnts′] **82** 6

blush [blŭsh] **23** 32

board [börd] **82** 16

boarding [bör′dĭng] **56**

boarding pass [bör′dĭng păs′] **56** 18

boardwalk [börd′wök′] **90** 1

body [bŏ′dē] **4**

boil [boyl] **31** 16

bollard [bŏl′ərd] **58** 26

bolt [bōlt] **36** 38

bomb [bŏm] **48** 3

bomber [bŏm′ər] **48** 2

bongos [bŏng′gōz] **98** 22

book [book] **12** 17

(book of) matches [book′ əv mă′chəz] **16** 28

bookcase [book′kās′] **28** 22, **83** 20

bookstore [book′stör′] **44** 18

boom [boom] **59** 7

booth [booth] **16** 9

boots [boots] **19** 21, **20** 32

bottle [bŏt′əl] **12** 3, **33** 17

bottle opener [bŏt′əl ō′pə nər] **30** 6

bounce [bowns] **96** 11

bow [bō] **98** 7a

bow [bow] **58** 5

bowl [bōl] **12** 23

bowling [bōl′ĭng] **94**

bowling ball [bōl′ĭng böl′] **94** 6

box [bŏks] **12** 12

box seat [bŏks′ sēt′] **99** 11

box spring [bŏks′ sprĭng′] **32** 18

boxer shorts [bŏk′sər shörts′] **22** 2

boxing [bŏk′sĭng] **94**

buoy [boo′ē] **58** 16

boy's frame [boyz′ frām′] **52** 11

bra(ssiere) [brŏ]/[brə zïr′] **22** 13

brace [brās] **36** 9

bracelet [brās′lət] **23** 9

brain [brān] **4** 57

brake [brāk] **50** 26, **52** 29

brake light [brāk′ līt′] **50** 29

branch [brănch] **60** 35a

brass [brās] **98**

bread [brĕd] **14** 12

bread and butter plate
[brĕd′ ənd bŭt′ ər plāt′] **29** 11

break [brāk] **31** 7

breast [brĕst] **10** 21

bricks [brĭks] **82** 12

bridle path [brīd′əl păth′] **87** 7

briefcase [brēf′kās′] **20** 37

briefs [brēfs] **22** 12

broccoli [brŏk′ə lē] **6** 2

broil [broyl] **31** 13

broiler [broy′lər] **30** 33

broken bone [brō′kən bōn′] **40** 15

broom [brŏŏm] **35** 7

brother [brŭdh′ər] **3** 9

brother-in-law [brŭdh′ər ən lö′] **3** 11

bruise [brŏŏz] **40** 17

brush [brŭsh] **76** 18

brussels sprouts [brŭs′əl sprowts′] **6** 4

bucket [bŭk′ət] **35** 15

bucket seat [bŭk′ət sēt′] **50** 16

buckle [bŭk′əl] **20** 17

bud [bŭd] **60** 18a

buffet [bə fā′] **29** 29

builder [bĭl′dər] **82** 5

building number [bĭl′dĭng nŭm′ bər]
44 24

bulb [bŭlb] **60** 8a

bull [bŏŏl] **66** 34

bulldozer [bŏŏl′dō′zər] **82** 27

bullet [bŏŏl′ĭt] **48** 26

bulletin board [bŏŏl′ĭ tən börd′] **76** 7

bumper [bŭm′pər] **33** 5

bun [bŭn] **18** 7

bunch [bŭnch] **8** 1

Bunsen burner [bŭn′sən bür′nər]
78 20

buoy [boy] **58** 16

bureau [byŏŏr′ō] **32** 9

burn [bürn] **17** 14, **40** 18

burner [bür′nər] **30** 29

bus [bŭs] **53** 20, **54**

bus driver [bŭs′ drī′vər] **54** 3

bus stop [bŭs′ stŏp′] **44** 13

busboy [bŭs′boy′] **16** 3

bushes [bŏŏsh′əz] **60** 41

business workers [biz′nəs wür′kərz] **86**

butcher [bŏŏ′chər] **84** 13

butter [bŭt′ər] **18** 18

buttercup [bŭt′ər kŭp′] **60** 17

butterfly [bŭt′ər flī′] **63** 3

buttocks [bŭt′əks] **4** 15

button [bŭt′ən] **20** 3, **101** 9

buttonhole [bŭt′ən hōl′] **101** 8

C-clamp [sē′klămp′] **36** 2

cab driver [kăb′ drī′vər] **54** 26

cabbage [kăb′ĭj] **6** 3

cabin [kăb′ĭn] **56** 19

cabin cruiser [kăb′ĭn krŏŏ′zər] **59** 16

cabinet [kăb′ə nət] **30** 22

cable [kā′bəl] **52** 23

cable car [kā′bəl kär′] **54** 32

cactus [kăk′təs] **60** 40

calculator [kăl′kyə lā′tər] **83** 19,
100 34

calendar [căl′ən dər] **83** 9

calf [kăf] **4** 20, **66** 31

California [kăl′ə för′nyə] **72** 5

call card [köl′ kärd′] **47** 6

call number [köl′ nŭm′bər] **47** 7

call slip [köl′ slĭp′] **47** 12

camel [kăm′əl] **66** 33

camera [kăm′ər ə] **100** 8

cameraperson [kăm′ər ə pür′sən] **86** 10

camisole [kăm′ə sōl′] **22** 9

camp stove [kămp′ stōv′] **88** 25

camper [kăm′pər] **53** 16

campfire [kămp′fīr′] **88** 31

camping [kăm′pĭng] **88**

can [kăn] **12** 10

can opener [kăn′ ō′pə nər] **30** 4

canary [kə nĕr′ē] **64** 14

candle [kăn′dəl] **29** 27

candlestick [kăn′dəl stĭk′] **29** 28

canister [kăn′ə stər] **30** 15

canned goods [kănd′ gŏŏdz′] **14** 13

cannon [kăn′ən] **48** 11

canoe [kə nŏŏ′] **59** 2

cantaloupe [kăn′tə lōp′] **8** 36

canyon [kăn′yən] **88** 3

cap [kăp] **19** 2, **20** 43, **92** 11

capsule [kăp′səl] **41** 5

car [kär] **54** 9

card catalog [kärd′ kăt′ə lög] **47** 4

cardigan [kär′dī gən] **20** 26

cardinal [kärd′nəl] **64** 11

cargo [kär′gō] **58** 10

cargo area [kär′gō ĕr′ē ə] **57** 12

cargo bay [kär′gō bā′] **75** 9

cargo door [kär′gō dör′] **57** 13

Caribbean Sea [kăr′ə bē′ən sē′] **70** 20

carpenter [kär′pən tər] **85** 2

carpenter's rule [kär′pən tərz rŏŏl′] **36** 1

carrot(s) [kär′ət(s)] **6** 32

carry [kär′ē] **26** 16

carry-on bag [kär′ē ŏn băg′] **56** 2

cars [kärz] **50-51**

carton [kär′tən] **12** 1

cartridge needle [kär′trĭj nē′dəl] **100** 19

carve [kärv] **31** 6

cash register [kăsh′ rĕ′jə stər] **14** 21

cashew(s) [kăsh′ŏŏ(z)] **8** 27

cashier [kă shïr′] **14** 22

Caspian Sea [kăs′pē ən sē′] **70** 27

casserole dish [kăs′ə rōl dĭsh′] **30** 14

cassette [kə sĕt′] **100** 26

cassette deck [kə sĕt′ dĕk′] **100** 22

cast [kăst] **39** 5

cat [kăt] **68** 4

catch [kăch] **96** 4

catcher [kăch′ər] **92** 2, **93** 16

catcher's mask [kăch′ərz măsk′] **92** 3

catcher's mitt [kăch′ərz mĭt′] **92** 4

caterpillar [kăt′ər pĭl′ər] **63** 1

cattle [kăt′əl] **81** 20

Caucasus [kö′kə səs] **70** 45

cauliflower [köl′ə flow′ər] **6** 1

ceiling [sē′lĭng] **28** 2

ceiling fan [sē′lĭng făn′] **28** 1

celery [sĕl′ə rē] **6** 10

cello [chĕl′ō] **98** 9

cement [sə mĕnt′] **82** 10

cement mixer [sə mĕnt′ mĭk′ sər]
    82 25

cement truck [sə mĕnt′ trŭk′] **49** 13

center [sĕn′tər] **79** 13, **93** 9

center divider [sĕn′tər də vī′dər]
    53 18, **82** 24

center fielder [sĕn′tər fēl′dər] **93** 2

center lane [sĕn′tər lān′] **53** 6

centerboard [sĕn′tər bōrd′] **59** 6

centipede [sĕn′tə pēd′] **63** 22

chain [chān] **23** 5, **52** 18

chair [chër] **29** 17

chalk [chŏk] **76** 10

chalk tray [chŏk′ trā′] **76** 9

chalkboard [chŏk′bōrd′] **76** 5

chandelier [shăn′də lïr′] **29** 3

change (the sheets) [chānj′dhə shēts′]
    38 13

changing table [chān′jĭng tā′bəl] **33** 9

charcoal briquettes
    [chär′kōl brĭ kĕts′] **27** 23

chart [chärt] **39** 10

check [chĕk] **14** 27, **16** 14

checked [chĕkt] **24** 18

checkout counter [chĕk′owt kown′tər]
    14 26

checkout desk [chĕk′owt dĕsk′] **47** 2

cheerleaders [chïr′lē′dərz] **93** 2

cheek [chĕk] **4** 35

cherries [chër′ēz] **8** 19

cherry picker [chër′ē pĭk′ər] **82** 18

chest [chĕst] **4** 12

chest of drawers [chĕst′əv drörz′]
    32 30

chestnut(s) [chĕs′nŭt(s)] **8** 32

chick [chĭk] **64** 22

chicken [chĭk′ən] **10** 24, **62** 23

child's seat [chīldz′sēt′] **50** 33

children [chĭl′drən] **2** 7

chills [chĭlz] **40** 4

chimney [chĭm′nē] **27** 9

chimpanzee [chĭm păn′zē] **68** 16

chin [chĭn] **4** 3

china [chī′nə] **29** 1

china closet [chī′nə klŏz′ət] **29** 2

chipmunk [chĭp′mŭnk] **66** 6

chop [chŏp] **26** 11, **31** 11

chops [chŏps] **10** 9, **10** 15

chorus [kör′əs] **99** 18

(chrysanthe)mum
    [krə săn′thə məm]/[mŭm] **60** 4

cigarette [sĭg′ə rĕt′] **16** 31

circle [sür′kəl] **79** 11

circuit breaker [sür′kət brā′kər] **35** 5

circular saw [sür′kyə lər sö′] **36** 20

circumference [sür kŭm′fə rəns] **79** 17

citrus fruits [sĭ′trəs frōōts′] **8**

city [sĭt′ē] **44-45**

clam(s) [klăm(z)] **10** 32

clamp [klămp] **78** 7

clarinet [klăr′ə nĕt′] **98** 16

clasp [klăsp] **23** 17

classroom [klăs′rōōm′] **76**

claw [klö] **62** 13a, **68** 2a

clean [klēn] **24** 6, **26** 2

cleanser [klĕn′zər] **35** 9

clear [klïr] **17** 6

cliff [klĭf] **88** 21

clip-on earring [klĭp′ŏn ïr′ĭng] **23** 15

clock [klŏk] **76** 2

close (v) [klōz] **77** 5

closed [klōzd] **24** 16

closet [klŏz′ət] **32** 3

cloth diaper [klöth′ dī′pər] **33** 13

clothes [klōz] **19-24**

clothesline [klōz′līn′] **35** 19

clothespins [klōz′pĭnz′] **35** 20

cloudy [klow′dē] **25** 2

clove [klōv] **6** 25a

cloverleaf [klō′vər lēf′] **53** 4

clubs [klŭbz] **95** 5

clutch [klŭch] **50** 25

coach [kōch] **93** 3

coal [kōl] **80** 7

coal mine [kōl′ mīn′] **80** 6

coaster [kō′stər] **16** 27

coat [kōt] **19** 24, **42** 13

cob [kŏb] **6** 12a

cobra [kō′brə] **65** 11

cockpit [kŏk′pĭt′] **56** 13

cockroach [kŏk′rōch′] **63** 9

cocktail lounge [kŏk′tāl lownj′] **16**

cocktail waitress [kŏk′tāl wā′trəs]**15** 32

cocoon [kə kōōn′] **63** 2

coconut [kō′kə nŭt′] **8** 3

coffee [kö′fē] **18** 35

coffeemaker [kö′fē mā′kər] **30** 31

coffeepot [kö′fē pŏt′] **29** 18

coffee table [kö′fē tā′bəl] **28** 26

coins [koynz] **12** 26

colander [kŏl′ən dər] **30** 7

cold [kōld] **25** 10, **40** 1

cold water faucet [kōld′ wŏ tər fö′sət]
    34 18

collar [kŏl′ər] **20** 20

colonial-style house
    [kə lō′nē əl stīl hows′] **27**

Colorado [kŏl′ə rŏd′ō] **72** 6

column [kŏl′əm] **50** 13

comb [kōm] **32** 6

combine (n) [kŏm′bīn] **81** 17

comet [kŏm′ət] **74** 2

comforter [kŭm′fər tər] **32** 22

command module [kə mănd′ mŏj′ōōl]
    75 8

communication satellite
    [kə myōō′nə kā shən săt′ə līt] **75** 2

commuter [kə myōō′tər] **54** 17

commuter train [kə myōō′tər trān′]
    54 14

compact disc (CD)
    [kŏm′păkt dĭsk′]/[sē′ dē′] **100** 27

compact disc player
    [kŏm′păkt dĭsk′ plā′ər] **100** 28

computer [kəm pyōō′tər] **76** 8, **83**
    16 **100**

computer programmer
    [kəm pyōō′tər prō′grăm ər] **86** 16

conductor [kən dŭk′tər] **54** 7, **99** 8

cone [kōn] **60** 34b, **79** 28, **82** 19

conga [kŏng′gə] **98** 20

Congo River [kŏng′gō rĭv′ər] **70** 62

Connecticut [kə nĕ′tĭ kət] **72** 7

constellation [kŏn′ stə lā′shən] **74** 3

construction [kən strŭk′shən] **82**

(construction) boots
    [kən strŭk′shən bōōts′] **20** 32

construction site [kən strŭk′shən sīt′] **82**

construction worker
    [kən strŭk′shən wür′kər] **82** 14

container [kən tā′nər] **12** 2, **58** 7

(container)ship [kən tā/nər shĭp/] **58** 9

containers [kən tā/nərz] **12**

continents [kŏn/tə nənts] **70**

control tower [kən trōl/tow/ər] **57** 20

conveyor belt [kən vā/ər bĕlt/] **14** 23,
    56 12

cook (n) [kŏok] **16** 1

cook (v) [kŏok] **17** 4

cookie [kŏok/ē] **18** 22

cool [kŏol] **25** 9

cooler [kŏo/lər] **90** 41

cooling tower [kŏo/lĭng tow/ər] **80** 16

copilot [kō/pī/lət] **56** 16

cord [körd] **32** 26a, **54** 1

(corduroy) pants [kör/də roy pănts/]
    20 27

core [kör] **8** 2b, **80** 14

cork [körk] **16** 18

corkscrew [körk/skrŏo/] **16** 17

corn [körn] **6** 12, **60** 24

corner [kör/nər] **44** 3

corral [kə răl/] **81** 24

cosmetics [kŏz mĕt/ĭks] **23**

cotton balls [kŏt/ən bölz/] **39** 23

cotton swab [kŏt/ən swöb/] **33** 10

counter [kown/tər] **30** 27

court [kört] **43**, **94** 13

court officer [kört/ ö/fə sər] **43** 19

court reporter [kört/ rə pör/tər] **43** 14

cousin [kŭz/ən] **3** 7

cow [kow] **66** 32

cowboy [kow/boy/] **81** 21

cowgirl [kow/gürl/] **81** 22

crab(s) [krăb(z)] **10** 36, **62** 9

cradle [krā/dəl] **33** 26

cranberries [krăn/bĕr/ēz] **8** 13

crane [krăn] **58** 6

creamer [krē/mər] **29** 24

crew [krŏo] **75** 12

(crewneck) sweater
    [krŏo/nĕk swĕt/ər] **19** 7

crib [krĭb] **33** 4

cricket [krĭk/ət] **63** 5

crime [krīm] **43**

crochet [krō/shā/] **101** 28

crochet hook [krō/shā/ hŏok/] **101** 29

crocus [krō/kəs] **60** 9

cross-country skiing
    [krös/ kŭn trē skē/ĭng] **94**

crosswalk [krös/wök/] **44** 4

crow [krō] **64** 3

crutch [krŭch] **39** 7

cube [kyŏob] **79** 27

cubicle [kyŏo/bə kəl] **83** 5

cucumber(s) [kyŏo/kŭm bər(z)] **6** 20

cuff links [kŭf/ lĭnks/] **23** 12

cup [kŭp] **12** 19, **29** 20

curb [kürb] **44** 26

curtain [kür/tən] **32** 10, **99** 1

curtain rings [kür/tən rĭngz/] **34** 2

curtain rod [kür/tən rŏd/] **34** 1

curve [kürv] **79** 3

cushion [kŏosh/ən] **28** 24

customer [kŭs/tə mər] **14** 17

cut (v) [kŭt] **31** 9

cut (n) [kŭt] **40** 16

cutting board [kŭt/ĭng börd/] **30** 26

cylinder [sĭl/ĭn dər] **79** 26

cymbals [sĭm/bəlz] **98** 18

daffodil [dăf/ə dĭl] **60** 8

dairy cow [dër/ē kow/] **81** 11

dairy farm [dër/ē färm/] **81**

dairy products [dër/ē prŏd/ŭkts] **14** 4

daisy [dā/zē] **60** 5

dam [dăm] **80** 18

dance [dăns] **99**

dancer [dăn/sər] **99** 3

dark [därk] **24** 10

dashboard [dăsh/börd/] **50** 19

date [dāt] **8** 22

daughter [dö/tər] **3** 15

deck [dĕk] **27** 5, **58** 22

deer [dïr] **66** 26

defendant [də fĕn/dənt] **43** 23

defense attorney [də fĕns/ ə tür/nē]
    43 22

Delaware [dĕl/ə wär/] **72** 8

deli counter [dĕl/ē kown/tər] **14** 1

delivery boy [də lĭv/ə rē boy/] **85** 10

delivery person [də lĭv/ə rē pür/ sən]
    49 17

dental care [dĕn/təl kër/] **39**

dentist [dĕn/tĭst] **39** 17

department store [də pärt/mənt stör/]
    44 5

depth [dĕpth] **79** 33

derrick [dĕr/ĭk] **80** 2

deserts [dĕz/ərts] **70**

desk [dĕsk] **28** 14, **76** 16, **83** 13

detective [də tĕk/tĭv] **43** 2

diagonal [dī ăg/ə nəl] **79** 20

diameter [dī ăm/ə tər] **79** 12

dictionary [dĭk/shə nër/ē] **47** 24

diesel fuel [dē/zəl fyŏo/əl] **80** 34

dig [dĭg] **26** 3

dime [dīm] **12** 29

dinghy [dĭng/ē] **59** 18

dining room [dī/nĭng rŏom/] **29**

dipstick [dĭp/stĭk/] **50** 58

dirt bike [dürt/ bīk/] **52** 8

disc jockey (DJ) [dĭsk/ jŏk/ē] / [dē/jā/]
    86 9

dirty [dür/tē] **24** 5

dish drainer [dĭsh/ drā/nər] **30** 2

dish towel [dĭsh/ tow/əl] **30** 18

dishwasher [dĭsh/wŏsh/ər] **30** 1

dishwashing liquid
    [dĭsh/wŏsh ĭng lĭ/kwĭd] **30** 10

disposable diaper
    [dĭs pō/zə bəl dī/pər] **33** 12

dissection kit [dī sĕk/shən kĭt/] **78** 33

dive [dīv] **96** 14

dock [dŏk] **58** 28

doctor [dŏk/tər] **39** 11

dogs [dögz] **68**

dogwood [dög/wŏod/] **60** 28

doll [dŏl] **33** 28

doll house [dŏl/ hows/] **33** 25

dollar bills [dŏl/ər bĭlz/] **12** 25

dolly [dŏl/ē] **56** 6

dolphin [dŏl/fĭn] **68** 13

donkey [dŏng/kē] **66** 23

door handle [dör/ hăn/dəl] **50** 4

door lock [dör/ lŏk/] **50** 1

doorman [dör/mən] **85** 11

down [down] **103** 3

down vest [down/ vĕst/] **19** 12

dragonfly [drăg/ən flī/] **63** 4

drain [drān] **34** 9

drainpipe [drān/pīp/] **27** 18

drapes [drāps] **28** 23

draw [drö] **77** 11

drawer [drör] **47** 2

dress [drĕs] **20** 22

dried fruits [drīd/ frōōts/] **8**

drill [drĭl] **39** 15

drink [drĭngk] **17** 2

drive [drīv] **96** 15

driveway [drīv/wā/] **27** 1

drugstore [drŭg/stör/] **44** 22

drum [drŭm] **98** 19

drummer [drŭm/ər] **99** 27

drumsticks [drŭm/stĭks/] **98** 19a

dry [drī] **25** 14, **38** 9

dryer [drī/ər] **35** 24

duck [dŭk] **10** 25, **64** 25

(duck) pond [dŭk/ pŏnd/] **87** 8

dugout [dŭg/owt/] **93** 13

dump truck [dŭmp/ trŭk/] **49** 14

dust [dŭst] **38** 15

dustpan [dŭst/păn/] **35** 8

eagle [ē/gəl] **64** 5

ear [ïr] **4** 34

(ear of) corn [ïr/ əv körn/] **6** 12

earmuffs [ïr/mŭfs/] **19** 10

earrings [ïr/ĭngz] **23** 1

Earth [ürth] **74** 8, 13

east [ēst] **70** 73

East China Sea [ēst/ chī/nə sē/]
70 38

eat [ēt] **17** 1

eel [ēl] **65** 4

egg [ĕg] **18** 32, **64** 13

egg roll [ĕg/ rōl/] **18** 25

eggplant [ĕg/plănt/] **6** 21

elbow [ĕl/bō] **4** 8

electric drill [ĭ lĕk/trĭk drĭl/] **36** 43

electric guitar [ĭ lĕk/trĭk gĭ tär/]
99 26

electric generator
[ĭ lĕk/trĭk gĕn/ə rā tər] **80** 21

electrical tape [ĭ lĕk/trĭ kəl tāp/]
36 34

electrician [ĭ lĕk trĭ/shən] **85** 6

electricity [ĭ lĕk trĭs/ĭ tē] **80** 32

electronics [ĭ lĕk trŏn/ĭks] **100**

elephant [ĕl/ə fənt] **66** 17

elevator [ĕl/ə vā/tər] **44** 17, **80** 10

elm [ĕlm] **60** 36

embroidery [ĕm broi/də rē] **101** 27

emergency brake [ĭ mür/jən sē brāk/]
50 15

emery board [ĕm/ə rē börd/] **23** 24

encyclopedia [ĕn sī/klə pē/dē ə] **47** 25

end table [ĕnd/ tā/bəl] **28** 29

end zone [ĕnd/ zōn/] **93** 5

energy [ĕn/ər jē] **80**

engagement ring [ĕn gāj/mənt rĭng/]
23 3

engine [ĕn/jən] **50**, **52** 32

engineer [ĕn/jə nïr/] **54** 15

enter [ĕn/tər] **77** 14

entrance ramp [ĕn/trəns rămp/] **53** 21

envelope [ĕn/və lōp/] **46** 16, **83** 31

equator [ĭ kwā/tər] **70** 70

erase [ĭ rās/] **77** 3

eraser [ĭ rā/sər] **76** 11

escarole [ĕs/kə rōl/] **6** 7

esophagus [ĭ sŏf/ə gəs] **4** 61

eucalyptus [yōō/kə lĭp/təs] **60** 27

Europe [yŏŏr/əp] **70** 3

examining table [ĭg zăm/ə nĭng tā/bəl]
39 6

exhaust pipe [ĭg zöst/pīp/] **52** 33

exit ramp [ĕg/zĭt rămp/] **53** 2

exit sign [ĕg/zĭt sīn/] **53** 24

Express Mail (package)
[ĭk sprĕs/ māl păk/ĭj] **46** 23

extension cord [ĭk stĕn/shən körd/]
36 5

eye [ī] **4**

eye drops [ī/ drŏps/] **41** 10

eye shadow [ī/ shă/dō] **23** 30

eyebrow [ī/brow/] **4** 44

eyebrow pencil [ī/brow pĕn/səl]
23 26

eyelashes [ī/ lăsh/əz] **4** 46

eyelid [ī/lĭd/] **4** 45

eyeliner [ī/lī/nər] **23** 33

fabric softener [făb/rĭk sö/fə nər]
35 27

face [fās] **4** 1

face guard [fās/gärd/] **92** 15

factory work [făk/tə rē würk/] **85**

fairway [fër/wā/] **95** 12

fall [föl] **96** 7

Fall [föl] **27**

family [făm/ə lē] **3**

family restaurant [făm/ə lē rĕs/tər ənt]
16

fan belt [făn/ bĕlt/] **50** 53

fare [fër] **54** 21

fare box [fër/ bŏks/] **54** 5

farmhouse [färm/hows/] **81** 3

farmer [fär/mər] **81** 7

farming [fär/mĭng] **81**

fashion designer [făsh/ən də zī/nər]
86 6

father [fŏdh/ər] **3** 5

faucet [fö/sĭt] **34** 16

fawn [fön] **66** 27

feather [fĕdh/ər] **64** 7a

feather duster [fĕdh/ər dŭs/tər] **35** 2

fence [fĕns] **81** 9

fender [fĕn/dər] **52** 10

ferry [fër/ē] **58** 17

fever [fē/vər] **40** 2

field [fēld] **81** 16

fields and courses [fēldz/ ənd kör/səz]
95

fig [fĭg] **8** 21

fighter plane [fī/tər plān/] **48** 1

file cabinet [fīl/ kăb/ə nət] **83** 21

file clerk [fīl/ klürk/] **83** 23

file folder [fīl/ fōl/dər] **83** 22

filet [fĭ lā/] **10** 28

fill [fĭl] **26** 9

film [fĭlm] **100** 10, **100** 17

filter paper [fĭl/tər pā/pər] **78** 16

fin [fĭn] **65** 3b

finger [fĭng/gər] **4** 25

fingernail [fĭng/gər nāl/] **4** 23

fingerprints [fĭng/gər prĭnts/] **43** 24

finish line [fĭn/ĭsh līn/] **95** 21

fire [fīr] **28** 9, **42** 5

fire engine [fīr/ ĕn/jən] **42** 2

fire escape [fīr/ ə skāp/] **42** 4

fire extinguisher
[fīr/ ĭk stĭng/gwĭ shər] **42** 11

fire fighter [fīr/ fī/tər] **42** 10

fire hydrant [fīr/ hī/drənt] **42** 9

fire truck [fīr/ trŭk/] **42** 3

firefighting [fīr/fī/tĭng] **42**

firefly [fīr/flī/] **63** 17

fireplace [fīr/plās/] **28** 8

first baseman [fürst/ bās/mən] **93** 8

first quarter [fürst/ kwör/tər] **74** 23

fish [fĭsh] **10** 26, **65**

fisherman [fĭsh/ər mən] **58** 3

fishing [fĭsh/ĭng] **88**

fishing boat [fĭsh/ĭng bōt/] **58** 1

fishing line [fĭsh/ĭng līn/] **88** 8

fishing net [fĭsh/ĭng nĕt/] **88** 9

fishing rod [fĭsh/ĭng rŏd/] **88** 7

flag [flăg] **76** 1, **82** 20, **95** 9

flame [flām] **29** 26, **78** 21

flamingo [flə mĭng/gō] **64** 29

flanker [flăng/kər] **93** 13

flannel shirt [flăn/əl shürt/] **19** 3

flare [flër] **50** 41

flash [flăsh] **100** 7

flashlight [flăsh/līt/] **35** 3

flask [flăsk] **78** 2

(flat) sheet [flăt/shēt/] **32** 19

flatbed [flăt/bĕd/] **49** 18

flight attendant [flīt/ ə tĕn/dənt] **56** 20

flight deck [flīt/dĕk/] **75** 10

flight engineer [flīt/ ĕn jə nïr/] **56** 17

flipper [flĭp/ər] **68** 12a

flippers [flĭp/ərz] **90** 36

floor [flör] **32** 29

Florida [flör/ə də] **72** 9

florist [flör/ĭst] **84** 11

flounder [flown/dər] **65** 7

flowers [flow/ərz] **60**

flute [flōōt] **99** 13

fly [flī] **63** 18

flying mammals [flī/ĭng mă/məlz] **66**

foal [fōl] **66** 22

foggy [fög/ē] **25** 12

fold [fōld] **38** 1

food [fōōd] **6–18**

foot [fōōt] **4**

football [fōōt/böl/] **92, 92** 13

football field [fōōt/böl fēld/] **93**

forceps [för/səps] **78** 28

forearm [för/ärm/] **4** 9

forehead [för/hĕd/] **4** 32

forelegs [för/lĕgz/] **66** 3d

foreman [för/mən] **85** 13

fork [förk] **29** 12

forklift [förk/lĭft/] **58** 4

foul line [fowl/līn/] **93** 9

foundation [fown dā/shən] **82** 11

four-door hatchback [för/dör hăch/băk] **50**

fox [fŏks] **68** 6

fractions [frăk/shənz] **79**

frame [frām] **28** 4

frame backpack [frām/ băk/păk] **88** 28

freezer [frē/zər] **14** 3, **30** 20

freezing [frē/zĭng] **25** 11

french fries [frĕnch/ frīz/] **18** 18

French horn [frĕnch/ hörn/] **98** 26

fried chicken [frīd/ chĭk/ən] **18** 29

Frisbee™ [frĭz/bē] **90** 18

frog [frŏg] **65** 17

from [frŭm] **103** 10

front bumper [frŭnt/ bŭm/pər] **50** 51

frozen foods [frō/zən fōōdz/] **14** 2

fruit and vegetable market
[frōōt/ ənd vĕj/tə bəl mär/kət] **45** 28

fruit tree [frōōt/ trē/] **81** 2

fruits [frōōts] **8**

fry [frī] **31** 15

frying pan [frī/ĭng păn/] **30** 5

fuel truck [fyōō/əl trŭk/] **49** 3

full moon [fōōl/ mōōn/] **74** 24

full slip [fōōl/ slĭp/] **22** 10

fullback [fōōl/băk/] **93** 16

funnel [fŭn/əl] **78** 17

fuselage [fyōō/sə lŏj/] **57** 14

galaxy [găl/ək sē] **74** 1

Ganges River [găn/jēz rĭv/ər] **70** 67

gangway [găng/wā/] **58** 20

garage [gə rŏj/] **27** 2

garbage can [gär/bĭj kăn/] **35** 31

garbage truck [gär/bĭj trŭk/] **49** 6

garden hose [gär/dən hōs/] **27** 14

gardenia [gär dēn/yə] **60** 14

gardener [gärd/nər] **85** 3

garlic [gär/lĭk] **6** 25

garment bag [gär/mənt băg/] **56** 1

garter belt [gär/tər bĕlt/] **22** 14

(garter) snake [gär/tər snāk/] **65** 9

gas gauge [găs/ gāj/] **50** 9

gas pump [găs/ pŭmp/] **53** 14

gas tank [găs/ tănk/] **50** 34

gas(oline) [găs/ə lēn/] **80** 28

(gauze) bandage [göz/ băn/dĭj] **39** 24

gauze pads [göz/ pădz/] **39** 25

gavel [găv/əl] **43** 12

gear [gïr] **88** 27

gear changer [gïr/ chān/jər] **52** 22

gearshift [gïr/shĭft/] **50** 17

geometrical figures
[jē/ ə mĕ/trĭ kəl fĭg/yərz] **79**

Georgia [jör/jə] **72** 10

geyser [gī/zər] **80** 5

gibbon [gĭb/ən] **68** 15

gill [gĭl] **65** 3c

giraffe [jə răf/] **66** 29

girdle [gür/dəl] **22** 15

girl [gürl] **2** 9

girl's frame [gürlz/ frām/] **52** 3

give [gĭv] **17** 9

glass [glăs] **12** 20

glasses [glăs/əz] **20** 44

glider [glī/dər] **57** 4

globe [glōb] **47** 19

glove [glŭv] **92** 12, **94** 11, **94** 15

glove compartment
[glŭv/ kəm pärt/mənt] **50** 20

gloves [glŭvz] **19** 1

glue [glōō] **37** 33, **76** 17

goal [gōl] **92** 25

goalie [gōl/ē] **92** 24

goalpost [gōl/pōst/] **93** 17

goat [gōt] **66** 28

Gobi Desert [gō/bē dĕz/ərt] **70** 54

golf [gŏlf] **94**

golf bag [gŏlf/ băg/] **95** 7

golf ball [gŏlf/ böl/] **94** 7

golf cart [gŏlf/ kärt/] **95** 8

golf course [gŏlf/ körs/] **95**

golfer [gŏl/fər] **94** 10

goose [gōōs] **64** 26

gooseberries [gōōs/bĕr/ēz] **8** 1

gopher [gō/fər] **66** 8

gorilla [gə rĭl/ə] **68** 17

graduated cylinder
[grăj/ōō ā tĭd sĭl/ən dər] **78** 25

grains [grānz] **60**

granddaughter [grănd/dö/tər] **2** 11

grandfather [grănd/fŏ/dhər] **3** 2

grandmother [grănd/mŭ/dhər] **3** 1

grandparents [grănd/păr/ənts] **2** 10

grandson [grănd/sŭn/] **2** 12

grapefruit [grāp/frōōt/] **8** 7

grapes [grāps] **8** 1

graph paper [grăf/ pā/pər] **78** 11

grass [grăs] **27** 15

grasses [grăs/əz] **60**

grasshopper [grăs/hŏp/ər] **63** 6

grate [grāt] **31** 2

Great Sandy Desert
  [grāt/ săn/dē dĕz/ərt] **70** 55

green [grēn] **95** 10

greengrocer [grēn/grŏ/sər] **84** 7

grill [grĭl] **27** 22, **88** 12

grizzly bear [grĭz/lē bër/] **68** 23

groceries [grŏ/sə rēz] **14** 24

ground beef [grownd/ bēf/] **10** 2

grounding plug [grown/dĭng plŭg/]
  36 7

guitar [gĭ tär/] **98** 11

Gulf of Alaska [gŭlf/ əv ə lăs/kə]
  70 17

Gulf of Guinea [gŭlf/ əv gĭn/ē] **70** 25

Gulf of Mexico [gŭlf/ əv mĕk/sə kō]
  70 19

gulfs [gŭlfs] **70**

gun [gŭn] **43** 7

gun turret [gŭn/ tür/ət] **48** 12

gutter [gŭt/ər] **27** 10, **94** 3

gymnast [jĭm/nəst] **94** 23

gymnastics [jĭm năs/tĭks] **94**

hacksaw [hăk/sö/] **36** 18

hair [hër] **4** 30

hair dryer [hër/ drī/ər] **34** 26

hairbrush [hër/brŭsh/] **32** 7

hairdresser [hër/drĕs/ər] **84** 10

half (1/2) [hăf] **79** 30

half slip [hăf/ slĭp/] **22** 8

halfback [hăf/băk/] **93** 15

hall [höl] **76** 12

ham [hăm] **10** 12

hamburger [hăm/bür/gər] **18** 9

hammer [hăm/ər] **36** 13

hammock [hăm/ək] **27** 11

hamper [hăm/pər] **34** 28

hand [hănd] **4**

hand brake [hănd/ brāk/] **52** 24

hand grenade [hănd/ grə nād/] **48** 29

hand towel [hănd/ tow/əl] **34** 23

hand truck [hănd/ trŭk/] **87** 4

handball [hănd/böl/] **94**, **94** 12

handcuffs [hănd/kŭfs/] **43** 4

handicrafts [hăn/dē krăfts/] **101**

handlebars [hăn/dəl bärz/] **52** 2

hang [hăng] **38** 6

hang glider [hăng/ glī/dər] **57** 6

hangar [hăng/ər] **57** 17

hanger [hăng/ər] **32** 2

hard hat [härd/ hăt/] **20** 28, **82** 4

harmonica [här mŏn/ə kə] **98** 30

harness [här/nəs] **88** 22

harp [härp] **98** 6

hat [hăt] **19** 18

hatchback [hăch/băk/] **50** 43

hatchet [hăch/ət] **36** 17

Hawaii [hə wŏ/ē] **72** 11

hawk [hök] **64** 7

hay [hā] **81** 13

hazelnut(s) [hā/zəl nŭt(s)/] **8** 30

head [hĕd] **4**, **37** 42a

(head of) cauliflower
  [hĕd/ əv köl/ə flow/ər] **6** 1

head protector [hĕd/ prə tĕk/tər] **94** 14

headache [hĕd/āk/] **40** 6

headboard [hĕd/börd/] **32** 14

headlights [hĕd/līts/] **50** 48

headphones [hĕd/fōnz/] **100** 29

headrest [hĕd/rĕst/] **50** 35

headset [hĕd/sĕt/] **83** 2

heart [härt] **4** 64

heat [hēt] **80** 27

heating pad [hē/tĭng păd/] **41** 3

hedge clippers [hĕj/ klĭp/ərz] **27** 29

heel [hēl] **4** 50, **20** 5

heels [hēlz] **21** 27

height [hīt] **79** 34

helicopter [hĕl/ə kŏp/tər] **57** 2

helmet [hĕl/mət] **42** 12, **52** 7, **92** 14

hem [hĕm] **101** 11

hem binding [hĕm/ bīn/dĭng] **101** 12

herb(s) [ürb(z)] **6** 9

(herd of) cattle [hürd/ əv kăt/əl] **81** 20

high [hī] **24** 11

high blood pressure [hī/ blŭd/ prĕsh/ər]
  40 10

high chair [hī/ chër/] **16** 8

high heels [hī/ hēlz/] **20** 25

highway travel [hī/wā trăv/əl] **53**

hikers [hī/kərz] **88** 2

hiking boots [hī/kĭng bōōts/] **19** 9

hill [hĭl] **88** 4

Himalayas [hĭm/ə lā/əz] **70** 47

hind legs [hīnd/ lĕgz/] **66** 3b

hip [hĭp] **4** 16

hippopotamus [hĭp/ə pŏt/ə məs] **66** 14

hit [hĭt] **96** 1

hitchhiker [hĭch/hī/kər] **53** 9

hockey stick [hŏk/ē stĭk/] **92** 18

hog [hög] **66** 30

hold [hōld] **17** 12, **58** 8

hole [hōl] **94** 8

holly [hŏl/ē] **60** 37

holster [hōl/stər] **43** 8

home plate [hōm/ plāt/] **93** 15

honeydew melon
  [hŭn/ē dōō mĕl/ən] **8** 35

hood [hŏŏd] **50** 47

hoof [hŏŏf] **66** 35b

hoofed mammals [hŏŏft/ măm/əlz] **66**

hook [hŏŏk] **32** 1, **36** 16

hook and eye [hŏŏk/ ənd ī/] **101** 14

horn [hörn] **50** 12, **52** 5, **66** 16a

horse [hörs] **66** 21

horse racing [hörs/ rā/sĭng] **94**

horse-drawn carriage
  [hörs/drön kăr/ĭj] **54** 33

horseback rider [hörs/băk rī/dər] **87** 6

horses [hörs/əz] **81** 23

hose [hōz] **42** 8, **50** 57

hot [hŏt] **25** 7

hot air balloon [hŏt/ ër bə lōōn/] **57** 1

hot dog [hŏt/ dög/] **18** 2

hot water faucet [hŏt/ wŏt ər fö/sət]
  34 17

house plants [hows/ plănts/] **60** 39

household items [hows/hōld ī/təmz]
  14 15

household services
[hows/hōld sür/və səz] **85**

housekeeper [hows/kē/pər] **85** 8

houses [how/zəz] **26**

housework [hows/würk/] **38**

Huang River [hwöng/ rĭv/ər] **70** 68

hubcap [hŭb/kăp/] **50** 36

Hudson Bay [hŭd/sən bā/] **70** 18

human body [hyoo/mən bŏd/ē] **4**

hummingbird [hŭm/ĭng bürd/] **64** 2

hump [hŭmp] **66** 33a

husband [hŭz/bənd] **2** 3, **3** 12

hyacinth [hī/ə sĭnth] **60** 10

hyena [hī ē/nə] **68** 30

hypotenuse [hī pŏt/ə noos/] **79** 24

ice cream cone [īs/ krēm cōn/] **18** 36

ice hockey [īs/ hŏk/ē] **92**

ice pack [īs/ păk/] **41** 4

ice skates [īs/ skāts/] **19** 15

ice skating [īs/ skā/tĭng] **94**

ice tray [īs/ trā/] **30** 21

icy [ī/sē] **25** 16

Idaho [ī/də hō/] **72** 12

ignition [ĭg nĭsh/ən] **50** 14

iguana [ĭ gwŏ/nə] **65** 13

Illinois [ĭl/ə noy/] **72** 13

in [ĭn] **102** 7

in front of [ĭn frŭnt/ əv] **102** 6

in-box [ĭn/bŏks] **83** 12

(index) finger [ĭn/dĕks fĭng/gər] **4** 25

Indian [ĭn/dē ən] **70** 13

Indiana [ĭn/dē ăn/ə] **72** 14

individual sports
[ĭn/də vĭj/ oo əl spörts/] **94**

infection [ĭn fĕk/shən] **40** 14

inflatable raft [ĭn flā/tə bəl răft/] **59** 20

information desk
[ĭn/fər mā/shən dĕsk/] **47** 22

injection [ĭn jĕk/shən] **41** 8

injuries [ĭn/jə rēz] **40**

insect bite [ĭn/sĕkt bīt/] **40** 3

insects [ĭn/sĕkts] **63**

instep [ĭn/stĕp/] **4** 51

instruments [ĭn/strə mənts]
39 13, **56** 14, **98**

internal organs [ĭn tür/nəl ör/gənz] **4**

intersection [ĭn/tər sĕk/shən] **44** 11

interstate highway
[ĭn/tər stāt hī/wā] **53** 1

intestines [ĭn tĕs/tənz] **4** 67

into [ĭn/too] **103** 12

Iowa [ī/ə wə] **72** 15

iris [ī/rəs] **4** 47, **60** 11

iron (n) [ī/ərn] **35** 12

iron (v) [ī/ərn] **38** 11

ironing board [ī/ər nĭng börd/] **35** 13

jack [jăk] **32** 26b, **50** 38

jacket [jăk/ət] **19** 17, **20** 33

jackhammer [jăk/hăm/ər] **82** 22

jail [jāl] **43** 1

janitor [jăn/ə tər] **85** 9

jar [jär] **12** 9

jaw [jö] **4** 38

jeans [jēnz] **19** 6

jeep [jēp] **48** 9

jelly [jĕl/ē] **18** 31

jellyfish [jĕl/ē fĭsh/] **62** 12

jet engine [jĕt/ ĕn/jən] **57** 11

jet fuel [jĕt/ fyoo/əl] **80** 31

(jet) plane [jĕt/ plān/] **57** 18

jeweller [joo/ə lər] **84** 12

jewelry [joo/əl rē] **23**

jewelry box [joo/əl rē bŏks/] **32** 4

jigsaw [jĭg/sö] **36** 3

jockey [jŏk/ē] **94** 21

jogging path [jŏg/ĭng păth/] **87** 9

judge [jŭj] **43** 10

jukebox [jook/bŏks/] **16** 12

jump [jŭmp] **96** 8

jungle gym [jŭng/əl jĭm/] **87** 17

Jupiter [joo/pə tər] **74** 15

jury [joor/ē] **43** 21

jury box [joor/ē bŏks/] **43** 20

kangaroo [kăng/gə roo/] **66** 3

Kansas [kăn/zəs] **72** 16

Kara Sea [kär/ə sē/] **70** 31

kayak [kī/ăk] **59** 17

Kentucky [kĕn tŭk/ē] **72** 17

ketchup [kĕch/əp] **16** 4

kettledrum [kĕt/əl drŭm/] **98** 21

keyboard [kē/börd/] **98** 1a, **100** 33

keyboard player [kē/börd plā/ər] **99** 22

kickstand [kĭk/stănd/] **52** 9

kidney [kĭd/nē] **4** 70

kidney bean(s) [kĭd/nē bēn(z)/] **6** 13

kitchen [kĭch/ən] **30**

kite [kīt] **90** 22

kitten [kĭt/ən] **68** 5

knee [nē] **4** 19

knee socks [nē/ sŏks/] **22** 16

knife [nīf] **29** 15

knitting [nĭt/ĭng] **101** 22

knitting needle [nĭt/ĭng nē/dəl] **101** 25

knuckle [nŭk/əl] **4** 22

koala [kō ŏl/ə] **66** 1

label [lā/bəl] **46** 21

lacrosse [lə krös/] **92**

lacrosse stick [lə krös/ stĭk/] **92** 16

ladder [lăd/ər] **42** 1, **82** 8

ladybug [lā/dē bŭg/] **63** 14

lamb [lăm] **10** 13, **66** 24

lamp [lămp] **28** 28

lampshade [lămp/shād/] **28** 27

landing gear [lăn/dĭng gîr/] **57** 15

lane [lān] **94** 4

lantern [lăn/tərn] **88** 29

lapel [lə pĕl/] **20** 1

Laptev Sea [lăp/tĕv sē/] **70** 33

last quarter [lăst/ kwör/tər] **74** 25

launchpad [lönch/păd/] **75** 15

laundry [lön/drē] **35** 28

laundry basket [lön/drē băs/kət] **35** 29

laundry detergent [lön/drē də tür/jənt]
35 25

lawn mower [lön/ mō/ər] **27** 12

lead guitarist [lēd/ gĭ tär/ĭst] **99** 25

leaf [lēf] **60** 36a

leave [lēv] **77** 13

left fielder [lĕft/ fēl/dər] **93** 1

left guard [lĕft/ gärd/] **93** 8

left lane [lĕft/ lān/] **53** 5

left tackle [lĕft/ tăk/əl] **93** 7

leg [lĕg] **4** 17, **10** 14, **10** 20

(legal) pad [lē/gəl păd/] **83** 26

lemon [lĕm/ən] **8** 9

Lena River [lē/nə rĭv/ər] **70** 66

length [lĕngth] **79** 36

lens [lĕnz] **100** 6

leopard [lĕp/ərd] **68** 1

letter [lĕt/ər] **46** 7

letter carrier [lĕt/ər kăr/yər] **46** 3

lettuce [lĕt′əs] **6** 6

level [lĕv′əl] **82** 3

librarian [lī brër′ē ən] **47** 22

library card [lī′brër ē kärd′] **47** 3

library clerk [lī′brër ē klürk′] **47** 1

license plate [lī′səns plāt′] **50** 28

lid [lĭd] **30** 9

life jacket [līf′ jăk′ət] **59** 1

life preserver [līf′ prə zür′vər] **90** 9

lifeboat [līf′bōt′] **58** 19, **90** 10

lifeguard [līf′gärd′] **90** 6

lifeguard chair [līf′gärd chër′] **90** 8

light (v) [līt] **17** 13

light (adj) [līt] **24** 9

light switch [līt′ swĭch′] **32** 25

lightbulb [līt′bŭlb′] **35** 22

lighter [lī′tər] **16** 30

lighthouse [līt′hows′] **58** 14

lily [lĭl′ē] **60** 3

lima bean(s) [lī′mə bēn(z)′] **6** 16

lime [līm] **8** 10

line [līn] **58** 25

lines [līnz] **79**

linesman [līnz′mən] **82** 17

lion [lī′ən] **68** 3

lip [lĭp] **4** 43

lipstick [lĭp′stĭk′] **23** 29

liquor (bottle) [lĭk′ər bŏt′əl] **16** 22

listen [lĭs′ən] **77** 6

little finger [lĭt′əl fĭng′gər] **4** 28

little league baseball [lĭt′əl lēg bās′böl] **92**

Little Leaguer [lĭt′əl lēg′ər] **92** 8

little toe [lĭt′əl tō′] **4** 55

liver [lĭv′ər] **4** 65

livestock [lĭv′stŏk′] **81** 12

living quarters [lĭv′ĭng kwör′tərz] **75** 11

living room [lĭv′ĭng rōōm′] **28**

lizard [lĭz′ərd] **65** 15

llama [lŏm′ə] **66** 15

loaf [lōf] **12** 7

loafer [lō′fər] **20** 42

lobby [lŏb′ē] **44** 2

lobster [lŏb′stər] **11** 30, **62** 13

lock [lŏk] **52** 13

locker [lŏk′ər] **76** 6

locksmith [lŏk′smĭth′] **85** 4

log [lög] **28** 10

long [löng] **24** 2

long johns [löng′ jŏnz′] **22** 7

long sleeve [löng′ slēv′] **20** 15

loose [lōōs] **24** 4

(loose-leaf) paper [lōōs′ lēf pā′ pər] **76** 13

loudspeaker [lowd′spē′kər] **76** 3

Louisiana [lōō ē′zē ăn′ə] **72** 18

lounge chair [lownj′ chër′] **27** 24

low [lō] **24** 12

lunar eclipse [lōō′nər ĭ klĭps′] **74** 6

lunar module [lōō′nər mŏj′ōōl] **75** 7

lunch box [lŭnch′ bŏks′] **20** 31

lunch truck [lŭnch′ trŭk′] **49** 8

lung [lŭng] **4** 63

machine gun [mə shēn′ gŭn′] **48** 25

magazine [măg′ə zēn′] **47** 16

magnet [măg′nət] **78** 27

magnifying glass [măg′nə fī ĭng glăs′] **78** 15

magnolia [măg nōl′yə] **60** 29

mail [māl] **46** 2

mail slot [māl′ slŏt′] **46** 13

mail truck [māl′ trŭk′] **46** 5

mailbag [māl′băg′] **46** 4

mailbox [māl′bŏks′] **46** 1

Maine [mān] **72** 19

maintenance [mān′tə nəns] **85**

make (the bed) [māk′ dhə bĕd′] **38** 8

makeup [māk′ŭp′] **23**

mallet [măl′ĭt] **36** 11

mammals [măm′əlz] **66-69**

man [măn] **2** 2

manager [măn′ĭ jər] **83** 18

mandolin [măn′də lĭn′] **98** 4

mane [mān] **66** 21a

mango [măng′gō] **8** 5

manhole [măn′hōl′] **44** 32

mantel [măn′təl] **28** 7

mantis [măn′tĭs] **63** 7

manual transmission [măn′yōō əl trănz mĭsh′ən] **50**

map [măp] **70**

maple [mā′pəl] **60** 38

marigold [măr′ə gōld′] **60** 6

marine [mə rēn′] **48** 18

Marines [mə rēnz′] **48** 17

Mars [märz] **74** 14

Maryland [mër′ə lənd] **72** 20

mascara [mă skăr′ə] **23** 28

mashed potatoes [măsht′ pə tā′tōz] **18** 17

mask [măsk] **90** 35

Massachusetts [măs′ə chōō′sĭts] **72** 21

mast [măst] **59** 8

mat [măt] **50** 22

matches [măch′əz] **16** 28

material [mə tïr′ē əl] **101** 4

math [măth] **79**

mattress [mă′trəs] **32** 16

measurement [mĕzh′ər mənt] **79**

meat [mēt] **10**

meatballs [mēt′bölz′] **18** 11

mechanic [mə kăn′ĭk] **84** 2

media [mē′dē ə] **86**

medical care [mĕd′ə kəl kër′] **39**

medicine [mĕd′ə sən] **41**

medicine chest [mĕd′ə sən chĕst′] **34** 14

medicine dropper [mĕd′ə sən drŏp′ər] **78** 26

Mediterranean Sea [mĕd′ĭ tə rā′nē ən sē′] **70** 24

melon [mĕl′ən] **6** 35

menu [mĕn′yōō] **16** 7

Mercury [mür′kyə rē] **74** 11

merry-go-round [mër′ē gō rownd′] **87** 5

message pad [mĕs′ĭj păd′] **83** 25

messenger [mĕs′ən jər] **86** 19

metal detector [mĕt′əl də tĕk′tər] **56** 10

meteor [mē′tē ər] **74** 5

meter [mē′tər] **54** 23

mezzanine [mĕz′ə nēn′] **99** 13

Michigan [mĭsh′ə gən] **72** 22

microfilm [mī′krə fĭlm′] **47** 13

microfilm reader [mī′krə fĭlm rē′dər] **47** 14

microscope [mī′krə skōp′] **78** 30

microwave oven [mī/krə wāv ŭv/ən] **30** 23

middle finger [mĭd/əl fĭng/gər] **4** 26

milk [mĭlk] **14** 5

Minicam™ [mĭn/ē kăm/] **100** 2

Minnesota [mĭn/ə sō/tə] **72** 23

mirror [mĭr/ər] **32** 5

Mississippi [mĭs/ə sĭp/ē] **72** 24

Mississippi River [mĭs/ə sĭp/ē rĭv/ər] **70** 58

Missouri [mĭ zŏŏr/ē] **72** 25

mitt [mĭt] **27** 20

mittens [mĭt/ənz] **19** 11

mixed vegetables [mĭkst/ vĕj/tə bəlz] **18** 16

mixing bowl [mĭk/sĭng bōl/] **30** 24

mobile [mō/bēl] **33** 2

model [mŏd/əl] **86** 5

Mojave Desert [mō hŏv/ē dĕz/ərt] **70** 48

money [mŭn/ē] **12**

money order [mŭn/ē ör/dər] **46** 18

monitor [mŏn/ə tər] **100** 32

monkey [mŭng/kē] **68** 14

monkey wrench [mŭng/kē rĕnch/] **36** 12

monorail [mŏn/ə rāl/] **54** 29

Montana [mŏn tăn/ə] **72** 26

Moon [mōōn] **74** 9

mooring [mŏŏr/ĭng] **59** 19

moose [mōōs] **66** 35

mop [mŏp] **35** 6

(mop) refill [mŏp/ rē/fĭl] **35** 11

mortar [mör/tər] **48** 28

mosquito [mə skē/tō] **63** 13

motel [mō tĕl/] **90** 3

moth [mŏth] **63** 21

mother [mŭdh/ər] **3** 4

motor oil [mōt/ər oyl/] **80** 33

motor scooter [mōt/ər skōō/tər] **52** 29

motorboat [mōt/ər bōt/] **59** 13

motorcycle [mōt/ər sī/kəl] **52** 30, **53** 19

mountain [mown/tən] **88** 19

mountain climbing [mown/tən klīm/ĭng] **88**

mountain ranges [mown/tən rān/jəz] **70**

mouse [mows] **66** 9

mouse trap [mows/ trăp/] **35** 32

mouth [mowth] **4** 2

mover [mōō/vər] **49** 12

movie camera [mōō/vē kăm/ə rə] **100** 15

moving van [mōō/vĭng văn/] **49** 11

mow [mō] **26** 6

mum [mŭm] **60** 4

muscle [mŭs/əl] **4** 62

mushroom(s) [mŭsh/rōōm(z)] **6** 30

music [myōō/zĭk] **99**

musical comedy [myōō/zə kəl kŏm/ə dē] **99**

musical instruments [myōō/zə kəl ĭn/strə mənts] **98**

musician [myōō zĭsh/ən] **99** 10

mussel(s) [mŭs/əl(z)] **10** 34, **62** 3

mustache [mŭs/tăsh] **4** 40

mustard [mŭs/tərd] **18** 1

nail [nāl] **36** 41

nail clippers [nāl/ klĭp/ərz] **23** 31

nail polish [nāl/ pŏl/ĭsh] **23** 25

nailbrush [nāl/brŭsh/] **34** 20

napkin [năp/kĭn] **29** 14

natural gas [năch/ər əl găs/] **80** 29

Navy [nā/vē] **48** 13

Nebraska [nə brăs/kə] **72** 27

neck [nĕk] **4** 4

necklace [nĕk/lĭs] **23** 6

nectarine [nĕk/tə rēn/] **8** 17

needle [nē/dəl] **39** 26, **60** 34a, **101** 18

needlecrafts [nē/dəl krăfts/] **101**

needlepoint [nē/dəl poynt/] **101** 26

neighborhood parks [nā/bər hŏŏd pärks/] **87**

nephew [nĕf/yōō] **3** 13

Neptune [nĕp/tōōn] **74** 18

nest [nĕst] **64** 31

net [nĕt] **92** 23

Nevada [nə văd/ə] **72** 28

new [nōō] **24** 13

New Hampshire [nōō/ hămp/shər] **72** 29

New Jersey [nōō/ jür/zē] **72** 30

New Mexico [nōō/ mĕk/sə kō] **72** 31

new moon [nōō/ mōōn/] **74** 26

New York [nōō/ yörk/] **72** 32

newscaster [nōōz/kăs/tər] **86** 2

newspaper [nōōz/pā/pər] **20** 48

newsstand [nōōz/stănd/] **44** 30

next to [nĕkst/ tōō] **102** 11

nickel [nĭk/əl] **12** 28

niece [nēs] **3** 14

Niger River [nī/jər rĭv/ər] **70** 61

night table [nīt/ tā/bəl] **32** 27

nightgown [nīt/gown/] **22** 21

nightstick [nīt/stĭk/] **43** 9

Nile River [nīl/ rĭv/ər] **70** 63

nipple [nĭp/əl] **33** 18

north [nörth] **70** 71

North America [nörth/ ə mĕr/ə kə] **70** 1

North Atlantic [nörth/ ăt lăn/tĭk] **70** 11

North Carolina [nörth/ kăr ə lī/nə] **72** 33

North Dakota [nörth/ də kō/tə] **72** 34

North Pacific [nörth/ pə sĭf/ĭk] **70** 9

North Sea [nörth/ sē/] **70** 21

nose [nōz] **4** 36, **57** 8

nostril [nŏs/trĭl] **4** 37

nozzle [nŏz/ əl] **42** 17

nuclear reactor [nōō/klē ər rē ăk/tər] **80** 13

nurse [nürs] **39** 19

nut [nŭt] **36** 39

nuts [nŭts] **8**

oak [ōk] **60** 33

oar [ör] **59** 22

oarlock [ör/lŏk/] **59** 21

oats [ōts] **60** 23

Ob River [ŏb/ rĭv/ər] **70** 64

oboe [ō/bō] **98** 15

obtuse angle [ŏb tōōs/ ăng/gəl] **79** 5

occupations [ŏk/yə pā/shənz] **84–86**

ocean liner [ō/shən lī/nər] **58** 27

oceans [ō/shənz] **70**

octopus [ŏk/tə pəs] **62** 6

office [ö/fĭs] **83**

office building [ö/fĭs bĭl/dĭng] **44** 1

officer [ö/fĭ sər] **86** 13

Ohio [ō hī/ō] **72** 35

oil [oyl] **38** 12

oil well [oyl/ wĕl/] **80** 1

ointment [oynt/mənt] **41** 9

Oklahoma [ō/klə hō/mə] **72** 36

old [ōld] **24** 14

on [ŏn] **102** 5

on top of [ŏn tŏp/ əv] **102** 10

onion(s) [ŭn/yən(z)] **6** 31

open [ō/pən] **24** 15, **31** 3

optician [ŏp tĭsh/ ən] **84** 9

oral hygienist [ör/əl hī jē/nĭst] **39** 14

orange [ör/ĭnj] **8** 8

orangutan [ə răng/ə tăn/] **68** 18

orbit [ör/bĭt] **74** 21

orchard [ör/chərd] **81** 1

orchestra [ör/kə strə] **99** 6

orchestra seating [ör/kə strə sēt/ ĭng] **99** 12

orchid [ör/kĭd] **60** 12

order [ör dər] **17** 5

Oregon [ör/ə gən] **72** 37

organ [ör/gən] **98** 29

ostrich [ŏs/trĭch] **64** 12

otter [ŏt/ər] **68** 10

out of [owt/ əv] **103** 7

outboard motor [owt/börd mō/tər] **59** 12

outer space [owt/ər spās/] **74**

outlet [owt/lət] **36** 6

oval [ō/vəl] **79** 18

oven [ŭv/ən] **30** 32

over [ō/vər] **103** 8

overalls [ō/vər ölz/] **20** 30

overcoat [ō/vər kōt/] **19** 20

overhead projector [ō/vər hĕd prə jĕk/tər] **76** 27

overpass [ō/vər păs/] **53** 3

owl [owl] **64** 6

oyster(s) [oy/stər(z)] **10** 33, **62** 2

pacifier [păs/ə fī/ər] **33** 22

pack [păk] **12** 16

package [păk/ĭj] **12** 4, **46** 19

pad [păd] **83** 26

paddle [păd/əl] **59** 3, **94** 18

pail [pāl] **90** 16

paint (v) [pānt] **26** 1

paint (n) [pānt] **36** 31

paintbrush [pānt/brŭsh/] **36** 30

Painted Desert [pān/təd dez/ərt] **70** 49

painter [pān/tər] **85** 7

painting [pān/tĭng] **28** 5

(pair of) scissors [për/ əv sĭz/ərz] **101** 17

pajamas [pə jŏm/əz] **22** 19

palm [pŏm] **4** 29, **60** 26

pan [păn] **36** 28

pancakes [păn/kāks/] **18** 5

pancreas [pang/krē əs] **4** 71

panda [păn də] **68** 20

panel truck [păn/əl trŭk/] **49** 9

pansy [păn/zē] **60** 2

panties [păn/tēz] **22** 11

pants [pănts] **20** 27

pantyhose [păn/tē hōz/] **22** 5

papaya [pə pī/yə] **8** 6

paper [pā/pər] **76** 13

paper clips [pā/pər klĭps/] **83** 28

paper towels [pā/pər tow/əlz] **35** 23

parachute [păr/ə shoot/] **48** 6

parakeet [păr/ə kēt] **64** 15

parallel lines [păr/ə lĕl līnz/] **79** 4

paramedic [păr/ə mĕd/ĭk] **42** 7

Parana River [păr/ə nŏ/ rĭv/ər] **70** 60

parents [păr/ənts] **2** 6

park [pärk] **87**

park ranger [pärk/ rān/jər] **88** 5

parking lights [pär/kĭng līts/] **50** 49

parka [pär/kə] **19** 8

parking garage [pär/kĭng gə rŏj/] **44** 19

parking meter [pär/kĭng mē/tər] **44** 20

parrot [păr/ət] **64** 16

part [pärt] **4** 31

pass [păs] **96** 5

passenger [păs/ĭn jər] **54** 25

passenger car [păs/ĭn jər kär/] **53** 15

pasture [păs/chər] **81** 6

patient [pā/shənt] **39** 20

patio [păt/ē ō/] **27** 17

pattern [păt/ərn] **101** 7

pattern piece [păt/ərn pēs/] **101** 6

paw [pö] **68** 29a

pay [pā] **17** 7

pea(s) [pē(z)] **6** 17

peach [pēch] **8** 37

peacock [pē/kŏk/] **64** 18

peak [pēk] **88** 20

peanut(s) [pē/nŭt(s)/] **8** 28

pear [për] **8** 18

pedal [pĕd/əl] **39** 18, **52** 19

pedestrian [pə dĕs/trē ən] **44** 12

peel (n) [pēl] **8** 20a

peel (v) [pēl] **31** 5

pegboard [pĕg/börd/] **36** 15

pelican [pĕl/ə kən] **64** 24

pencil [pĕn/səl] **76** 24

pencil eraser [pĕn/səl ə rā/sər] **76** 21

pencil sharpener [pĕn/səl shär/pə nər] **76** 20, **83** 30

Pennsylvania [pĕn səl vān/yə] **72** 38

penny [pĕn/ē] **12** 27

penguin [pĕn/gwĭn] **64** 27

people [pē/pəl] **2**

pepper shaker [pĕp/ər shā/kər] **29** 9

pepper(s) [pĕp/ər(z)] **6** 22

percussion [pər kŭsh/ən] **98**

perfume [pür/fyoom] **23** 27

periodicals section [pïr/ē ŏd/ə kəlz sĕk/shən] **47** 15

periscope [për/ə skōp/] **48** 8

perpendicular lines [pür/pən dĭk/yə lər līnz/] **79** 2

Persian Gulf [pür/zhən gŭlf/] **70** 28

personal computer (PC) [pür/sə nəl kŭm pyoo/tər]/ [pē/sē/] **100** 31

personnel [pür/sə nĕl/] **48**

petal [pĕt/əl] **60** 18b

petri dish [pĕt/rē dĭsh/] **78** 3

petunia [pə toon/yə] **60** 7

pharmacist [fär/mə sĭst] **84** 1

phases of the moon [fā/zəz əv dhə moon/] **74**

pheasant [fĕz/ənt] **64** 19

Phillips screwdriver [fĭl/ĭps skroo/drī vər] **36** 25

phone [fōn] **32** 26

photocopier [fō/tə kŏp/ē ər] **83** 24

photocopy machine [fō/tə kŏp ē mə shēn/] **47** 18

photographer [fə tŏg/rə fər] **86** 4

photography [fə tŏg/rə fē] **100**

piano [pē ăn/ō] **98** 1

piccolo [pĭk/ə lō/] **98** 2

pick (v) [pĭk] **26** 7

pick [pĭk] **98** 11a

pickup truck [pĭk/ŭp trŭk/] **49** 4

pickax [pĭk/ăks/] **82** 13

pickle [pĭk/əl] **18** 8

picnic area [pĭk/nĭk ër/ē ə] **88**

picnic basket [pĭk/nĭk băs/kət] **88** 13

picnic table [pĭk/nĭk tā/bəl] **88** 15

piece [pēs] **12** 22

pier [pïr] **58** 3

pierced earring [pïrst/ ïr/ĭng] **23** 16

pigeon [pĭj/ən] **64** 1

pill [pĭl] **41** 7

pillow [pĭl/ō] **32** 16

pillowcase [pĭl/ō kās/] **32** 15

pilot [pī/lət] **56** 14

pin [pĭn] **23** 8, **94** 5, **101** 20

pincushion [pĭn/kŏŏsh/ən] **101** 3

pine [pīn] **60** 34

pineapple [pīn/ăp/əl] **8** 4

ping-pong [pĭng/pŏng/] **94**

ping-pong ball [pĭng/pŏng böl/] **94** 19

pinking shears [pĭng/kĭng shïrz/] **101** 5

pipe [pīp] **16** 26, **35** 18

pipette [pī pĕt/] **78** 14

pit [pĭt] **8** 37a

pitcher [pĭch/ər] **29** 4, **92** 12

pitcher's mound [pĭch/ərz mownd/] **93** 11

pitchfork [pĭch/förk/] **81** 14

pizza [pēt/sə] **18** 30

plaid [plăd] **24** 22

plane [plān] **57** 18

planets [plăn/əts] **74**

plant (v) [plănt] **26** 4

plants (n) [plănts] **60**

plate [plāt] **29** 13

plateau [plă tō/] **88** 1

platform [plăt/förm/] **54** 11

playground [plā/grownd/] **87** 15

playpen [plā/pĕn/] **33** 30

pleasure boating [plĕzh/ər bō/tĭng] **59**

pliers [plī/ərz] **36** 19

plug [plŭg] **36** 43d

plum [plŭm] **8** 34

plumber [plŭm/ər] **85** 1

plunger [plŭn/jər] **35** 14

Pluto [plōō/tō] **74** 19

pocket [pŏk/ət] **20** 41

pod [pŏd] **6** 17a

podium [pō/dē əm] **99** 7

poinsettia [poyn sĕt/ē ə] **60** 15

poison ivy [poy/zən ī/vē] **60** 45

poison oak [poy/zən ōk/] **60** 43

poison sumac [poy/zən sōō/măk] **60** 44

poisonous plants [poy/zə nəs plănts/] **60**

polar bear [pōl/ər bër/] **68** 22

pole [pōl] **94** 34, **95** 14

police officer [pə lēs/ öf/ə sər] **43** 6

police station [pə lēs/ stā/shən] **43**

polish [pŏl/ĭsh] **38** 3

polka dot [pō/kə dŏt/] **24** 19

pond [pŏnd] **87** 8

pony [pō/nē] **66** 20

poplar [pŏp/lər] **60** 30

porch [pörch] **27** 6

porcupine [pör/kyə pīn/] **66** 11

pork [pörk] **10** 6

pork chops [pörk/chŏps/] **18** 15

port [pört] **58**

porter [pör/tər] **56** 5

porthole [pört/hōl/] **58** 21

post [pōst] **23** 18

post office [pōst/ öf/ĭs] **44** 9, **46**

postal worker [pōs/təl wür/kər] **46** 14

postcard [pōst/kärd/] **46** 17

postmark [pōst/märk/] **46** 9

pot [pŏt] **30** 13

pot holder [pŏt/hōl/dər] **30** 34

potato chips [pə tā/tō chĭps/] **18** 4

potato(es) [pə tā/tō(z)] **6** 23

potty [pŏt/ē] **33** 33

pouch [powch] **66** 3c

pouched mammals [powcht/ măm/əlz] **66**

poultry [pōl/trē] **10**

pour [pör] **31** 4

power lines [pow/ər līnz/] **80** 24

power sander [pow/ər săn/dər] **36** 26

power saw [pow/ər sö/] **27** 25

power station [pow/ər stā/shən] **80** 20

prepositions [prep/ə zĭ/shənz] **102, 103**

primates [prī/māts] **68**

print [prĭnt] **24** 21

printer [prĭn/tər] **83** 4

printout [prĭnt/owt/] **83** 8

prints [prĭnts] **100** 11

prism [prĭz/əm] **78** 1

private jet [prī/vət jĕt/] **57** 3

produce [prŏd/ōōs] **14** 9

programs [prō/grămz] **99** 17

projector [prə jĕk/tər] **100** 16

propane gas [prō/pān găs/] **80** 30

propeller plane [prə pĕl/ər plān/] **57** 7

prosecuting attorney [prŏ/sə kyōō tĭng ə tür/nē] **43** 17

prune [prōōn] **8** 23

public library [pŭb/lĭk lī/brër ē] **47**

public transportation [pŭb/lĭk trăns pər tā/shən] **54**

public telephone [pŭb/lĭk tĕl/ə fōn] **44** 7

puck [pŭk] **92** 17

pump [pŭmp] **12** 14, **52** 21

pumpkin [pŭmp/kĭn] **6** 26

punishment [pŭn/ĭsh mənt] **43**

pupil [pyōō/pəl] **4** 48

puppy [pŭp/ē] **68** 27

purse [pürs] **20** 23

push [pŏŏsh] **26** 12

putter [pŭt/ər] **94** 9

puzzle [pŭz/əl] **33** 31

pyramid [pïr/ə mĭd/] **79** 25

quantities [kwŏn/tə tēz] **12**

quarter [kwör/tər] **10** 18, **12** 30, **79** 31

quarterback [kwör/tər băk/] **93** 14

quill [kwĭl] **66** 11a

quilting [kwĭl/tĭng] **101** 32

rabbit [răb/ĭt] **66** 13

raccoon [ră kōōn/] **68** 7

race track [rās/ trăk/] **95**

(racing) handlebars [rā/sĭng hăn/dəl bärz] **52** 2

rack [răk] **47** 17, **78** 8

racket [răk/ĭt] **94** 2

racquet [răk/ĭt] **94** 29

racquetball [răk/ĭt böl/] **94** 30

radiator [rā/dē āt/ər] **50** 56

radio [rā/dē ō/] **50** 18

radish(es) [răd/ĭsh (əz)] **6** 29

radius [rā/dē əs] **79** 14

raft [răft] **88** 16

rafters [răf/tərz] **82** 1

rafting [răf/tĭng] **88**

rags [răgz] **35** 4

rain boots [rān/ boots/] **19** 25

raincoat [rān/kōt/] **20** 38

rainy [rān/ē] **25** 1

raise (one's hand) [rāz/ wŭnz hănd/]
   77 1

raisin(s) [rā/zən(z)] **8** 24

rake (v) [rāk] **26** 10

rake (n) [rāk] **27** 30

ranch [rănch] **81**

ranch house [rănch/ hows/] **27**

ranching [rănch/ĭng] **81**

rapids [răp/ĭdz] **88** 17

rash [răsh] **40** 1

raspberries [răz/bër/ēz] **8** 12

rat [răt] **66** 7

rattle [răt/əl] **33** 21

rattlesnake [răt/əl snāk/] **65** 10

razor [rā/zər] **23** 20

razor blades [rā/zər blādz/] **23** 23

read [rēd] **77** 4

real estate agent [rēl/ ə stāt ā/jənt]
   85 5

rear bumper [rïr/ bŭm/pər] **50** 42

rearview mirror [rïr/vyoo mïr/ər]
   50 7

receipt [rə sēt/] **14** 20, **54** 24

receiver [rə sē/vər] **100** 21

receptionist [rə sĕp/shə nəst] **86** 17

recliner [rə klī/nər] **28** 16

records [rĕk/ərdz] **100** 23

rectangle [rĕk/tăng/gəl] **79** 19

Red Sea [rĕd/ sē/] **70** 29

redwood [rĕd/wood/] **60** 25

(reel of) film [rēl/ əv fĭlm/] **100** 17

referee [rĕf/ə rē/] **93** 4, **94** 16

reference section
   [rĕf/ə rəns sĕk/shən] **47** 21

(reference) librarian
   [rĕf/ə rəns lī brër/e ən] **47** 22

refill [rē/fĭl/] **35** 11

refinery [rə fī/nə rē] **80** 12

reflector [rə flĕk/tər] **52** 25

refreshment stand
   [rə frĕsh/mənt stănd/] **90** 2

refrigerator [rə frĭj/ə rā/tər] **30** 19

reins [rānz] **94** 22

relationships [rə lā/shən shĭps/] **2**

remedies [rĕm/ə dēz] **41**

remote control [rə mōt/ kən trōl/]
   28 17

repair [rə për/] **38** 10

repairperson [rə për/pür/sən] **84** 5

reporter [rə pör/tər] **86** 11

reptiles [rĕp/tīlz] **65**

rescue [rĕs/kyoo] **42**

restaurant [rĕs/tə rənt] **16**

retriever [rə trē/vər] **68** 26

return address [rə türn/ ă drĕs/] **46** 8

rhinoceros [rī nŏs/ə rəs] **66** 16

Rhode Island [rōd/ ī/lənd] **72** 39

rice [rīs] **60** 21

ride [rīd] **96** 13

rider [rī/dər] **54** 6

rifle [rī/fəl] **48** 21

right angle [rīt/ ăng/gəl] **79** 23

right fielder [rīt/ fēl/dər] **93** 3

right guard [rīt/ gärd/] **93** 10

right lane [rīt/ lān/] **53** 7

right tackle [rīt/ tăk/əl] **93** 11

right triangle [rīt/ trī/ăng gəl] **79** 22

rind [rīnd] **8** 8b

ring(s) [rĭng(z)] **23** 2, **74** 16a, **94** 17

ring binder [rĭng/ bīn/dər] **76** 14

ring finger [rĭng/ fĭng/gər] **4** 17

ring stand [rĭng/ stănd/] **78** 19

rink [rĭngk] **94** 25

Rio Grande River [rē/ō grănd/ rĭv/ər]
   70 57

rivers [rĭv/ərz] **70**

road sign [rōd/ sīn/] **53** 23

road work [rōd/ würk/] **82**

roadrunner [rōd/rŭn/ər] **64** 32

roast [rōst] **10** 3, **10** 8

roasting pan [rōs/tĭng păn/] **30** 17

robes [rōbz] **43** 11

robin [rŏb/ĭn] **64** 9

rock group [rŏk/ groop/] **99**

rocket [rŏk/ət] **75** 13

rocks [rŏks] **88** 11

rocking chair [rŏk/ĭng chër/] **33** 16

Rocky Mountains [rŏk/ē mown/tənz]
   70 40

rodents [rō/dənts] **66**

roll [rōl] **12** 11, **18** 19

(roll of) film [rōl/ əv fĭlm/] **100** 10

roller [rōl/ər] **36** 29

rolling pin [rōl/ĭng pĭn/] **30** 25

rolodex [rōl/ə dĕks/] **83** 14

rooster [roo/stər] **64** 21

roof [roof] **27** 4

root [,root] **60** 35d

rope [rōp] **88** 23

rose [rōz] **60** 18

rotor [rō/tər] **57** 2

rough [rŭf] **95** 6

router [row/tər] **36** 37

row [rō] **47** 11, **81** 18

rowboat [rō/bōt/] **59** 23

Rub/al Khali Desert
   [roob/ ăl/ kŏl/ē dĕz/ərt] **70** 52

rubber tubing [rŭb/ər toob/ĭng] **78** 18

rudder [rŭd/ər] **59** 5

rug [rŭg] **32** 28

ruler [roo/lər] **76** 23

run [rŭn] **96** 6

rung [rŭng] **82** 9

runner [rŭn/ər] **90** 23, **94** 31

runway [rŭn/wā/] **57** 19

saddle [săd/əl] **94** 20

safety glasses [săf/tē glăs/əz] **78** 12

safety goggles [săf/tē gŏg/əlz] **94** 28

safety pin [săf/tē pĭn/] **33** 11

Sahara Desert [sə hër/ə dĕz/ərt] **70** 51

sail [sāl] **59** 9

sailboard [sāl/börd/] **59** 15

sailboat [sāl/bōt/] **59** 4

sailor [sāl/ər] **48** 14

salad bowl [săl/əd bōl/] **29** 25

salad dressing [săl/əd drĕs/ĭng] **18** 12

salamander [săl/ə măn/dər] **65** 14

salesperson [sālz/pür/sən] **86** 12

salt shaker [sölt′ shā′kər] **29** 10

sand (v) [sănd] **26** 14

sand (n) [sănd] **90** 31

sand dunes [sănd′ do͞onz′] **90** 12

sand trap [sănd′ trăp′] **95** 11

sandal [săn′dəl] **20** 19

sandbox [sănd′bŏks′] **87** 13

sandcastle [sănd′kăs′əl] **90** 32

sandpaper [sănd′pā′pər] **36** 27

sandwich [sănd′wĭch] **16** 16

sanitation worker
 [săn′ə tā′shən wür′kər] **49** 7

Saturn [săt′ərn] **74** 16

saucepan [sös′păn′] **30** 8

saucer [sö′sər] **29** 21

sausage [sö′sĭj] **10** 7

saw [sö] **36** 8

saxophone [săk′sə fōn′] **98** 24

scaffolding [skăf′əl dĭng] **82** 7

scale [skāl] **14** 7, **34** 32, **78** 4

scallop(s) [skăl′əp(s)] **10** 35, **62** 10

scarecrow [skĕr′krō′] **81** 19

scarf [skärf] **19** 19

scenery [sē′nə rē] **99** 1

school [sko͞ol] **76, 77**

science lab [sī′əns lăb′] **78**

scissors [sĭz′ərz] **101** 17

scoreboard [skör′börd′] **93** 1

scorpion [skör′pē ən] **63** 8

scouring pad [skowr′ĭng păd′] **30** 11

scrape [skrāp] **26** 15

scraper [skrāp′ər] **36** 14

screen [skrēn] **27** 19, **100** 14

screw [skro͞o] **36** 42

screwdriver [skro͞o′drī′vər] **36** 24

scrub [skrŭb] **38** 2

scuba tank [sko͞o′bə tăngk′] **90** 37

sea gull [sē′ gŭl′] **64** 6

sea horse [sē′ hörs′] **65** 1

Sea of Japan [sē′ əv jə păn′] **70** 36

Sea of Okhotsk [sē′ əv ō kŏtsk′]
 70 35

seafood [sē′fo͞od′] **10**

seal [sēl] **68** 12

seam [sēm] **101** 10

seas [sēz] **70**

seat [sēt] **52** 16, **54** 2

seat belt [sēt′ bĕlt] **50** 23

second baseman [sĕk′ənd bās′mən]
 93 7

secretary [sĕk′rə tĕr′ē] **83** 11

section [sĕk′shən] **8** 8a, **79** 15

security [sə kyo͝or′ə tē] **56**

security guard [sə kyo͝or′ə tē gärd′]
 56 9, **86** 14

sedan [sə dăn′] **50**

seed [sēd] **8** 8c

seesaw [sē′sö′] **87** 18

serve [sürv] **17** 3, **96** 2

service area [sür′vəs ër′ē ə] **53** 11

service court [sür′vəs kört′] **95** 1

service line [sür′vəs līn′] **95** 3

set (the table) [sĕt′ dhə tā′bəl] **17** 8

sewing [sō′ĭng] **101**

sewing machine [sō′ĭng mə shēn′]
 101 1

shade [shād] **33** 1

shaft [shăft] **80** 9

shampoo [shăm po͞o′] **34** 8

shank [shăngk] **37** 43b

shark [shärk] **65** 5

shaving cream [shā′vĭng krēm′] **23** 22

sheep [shēp] **66** 25, **81** 10

sheet [shēt] **32** 19

sheet music [shēt′ myo͞o′zĭk] **98** 2

shelf [shĕlf] **14** 6, **47** 26

shell [shĕl] **48** 27, **62** 1a, **65** 18a,
 90 40

shellfish [shĕl′fĭsh′] **10**

shepherd [shĕp′ərd] **68** 28

shingle [shĭng′gəl] **82** 2

ship [shĭp] **58** 9

shirt [shürt] **20** 46

shock absorbers [shŏk′ əb zör′ bərz]
 52 31

shoe [sho͞o] **20** 49

shoelace [sho͞o′lās′] **20** 7

shoot [sho͞ot] **96** 15

shop worker [shŏp′ wür′kər] **85** 12

shopping bag [shŏp′ĭng băg′] **20** 18

shopping basket [shŏp′ĭng bās′kət]
 14 8

shopping cart [shŏp′ĭng kärt′] **14** 19

short [shört] **24** 1

short sleeve [shört′ slēv′] **20** 21

shorts [shörts] **20** 14

shortstop [shört′stŏp′] **93** 5

shoulder [shōl′dər] **4** 5, **53** 22

(shoulder) bag [shōl′dər băg′] **20** 35

shovel (n) [shŭv′əl] **27** 31, **82** 15, **90** 17

shovel (v) [shŭv′əl] **26** 13

shower cap [show′ər kăp′] **34** 3

shower curtain [show′ər kür′tən] **34** 5

shower head [show′ər hĕd′] **34** 4

shrimp [shrĭmp] **10** 31, **62** 8

shutter [shŭt′ər] **27** 8

shuttle car [shŭt′əl kär′] **80** 8

side [sīd] **79** 10

side mirror [sīd′ mĭr′ər] **50** 2

sideburn [sīd′bürn′] **4** 33

sidewalk [sīd′wök′] **44** 25

Sierra Madre [sē ër′ə mŏ′drē] **70** 42

silo [sī′lō] **81** 4

silverware [sĭl′vər wër′] **29** 22

simple animals [sĭm′pəl ăn′ə məlz] **62**

singer [sĭng′ər] **99** 24

sink [sĭngk] **34** 19

sister [sĭs′tər] **3** 10

sister-in-law [sĭs′tər ən lö′] **3** 8

six-pack [sĭks′păk′] **12** 13

skate (n) [skāt] **94** 26

skate (v) [skāt] **96** 9

skein [skān] **101** 24

ski [skē] **95** 17

ski boot [skē′ bo͞ot′] **95** 15

ski cap [skē′ kăp′] **19** 16

ski lift [skē′ lĭft′] **95** 18

ski slope [skē′ slōp′] **95**

skiier [skē′ər] **94** 35

skis [skēz] **94** 33

skin [skĭn] **8** 37b

skirt [skürt] **20** 36

skunk [skŭngk] **68** 8

slacks [slăks] **20** 4

sleeping bag [slē′pĭng băg′] **88** 26

sleepwear [slēp′wër′] **22**

slice (n) [slīs] **12** 21

slice (v) [slīs] **31** 10

slide [slīd] **78** 31, **87** 12

slide projector [slīd′ prə jĕk′tər] **100** 13

slides [slīdz] **100** 12

sling [slĭng] **39** 3

slippers [slĭp⁄ərz] **22** 18

slug [slŭg] **62** 4

small [smöl] **24** 7

smoke [smōk] **42** 15

smoke detector [smōk⁄ də tĕk⁄tər] **33** 15

smokestack [smōk⁄stăk⁄] **58** 18, **80** 22

snacks [snăks] **14** 8

snail [snāl] **62** 1

snake [snāk] **65** 9

snap [snăp] **101** 13

sneakers [snē⁄kərz] **20** 11

snorkel [snör⁄kəl] **90** 34

snow plow [snō⁄ plow⁄] **49** 5

snowy [snō⁄ē] **25** 3

soap [sōp] **34** 15

soap dish [sōp⁄ dĭsh⁄] **34** 6

soccer [sŏk⁄ər] **92**

soccer ball [sŏk⁄ər böl⁄] **92** 26

socks [sŏks] **22** 17

sofa [sō⁄fə] **28** 25

soft drink [söft⁄ drĭngk⁄] **16** 11

softball [söft⁄böl⁄] **92**, **92** 10

solar collector [sō⁄lər kə lĕk⁄tər] **80** 17

solar eclipse [sō⁄lər ĭ klĭps⁄] **74** 10

solar system [sō⁄lər sĭs⁄təm] **74**

soldier [sōl⁄jər] **48** 16

sole [sōl] **20** 6

solid [sŏl⁄əd] **24** 20

solid figures [sŏl⁄əd fĭg⁄yərz] **79**

son [sŭn] **3** 16

Sony Walkman [sō⁄nē wök⁄mən] **100** 30

sore throat [sör⁄ thrōt⁄] **40** 12

south [sowth] **70** 72

South America [sowth⁄ ə mĕr⁄ə kə] **70** 2

South Atlantic [sowth⁄ ăt lăn⁄tək] **70** 12

South Carolina [sowth⁄ kăr ə lī⁄nə] **72** 40

South China Sea [sowth⁄ chi⁄nə sē⁄] **70** 39

South Dakota [sowth⁄ də kō⁄tə] **72** 41

South Pacific [sowth⁄ pə sĭf⁄ək] **70** 10

space probe [spās⁄ prōb⁄] **75** 4

space program [spās⁄ prō⁄grăm] **75**

space shuttle [spās⁄ shŭt⁄əl] **75** 14

space station [spās⁄ stā⁄shən] **75** 1

space suit [spās⁄ sōōt⁄] **75** 6

spacecraft [spās⁄krăft⁄] **75**

spaghetti [spə gĕt⁄ē] **18** 10

spaniel [spăn⁄yəl] **68** 24

spare ribs [spër⁄ rĭbz⁄] **10** 10

spare tire [spër⁄ tīr⁄] **50** 39

sparrow [spăr⁄ō] **64** 10

spatula [spăch⁄ə lə] **27** 21

speaker [spē⁄kər] **28** 21, **100** 24

speed limit sign [spēd⁄ lĭm ət sīn⁄] **53** 8

speedometer [spə dŏm⁄ə tər] **50** 10

spider [spī⁄dər] **63** 16

spinach [spĭn⁄əch] **6** 8

spinal cord [spī⁄nəl körd⁄] **4** 58

spiral notebook [spī⁄rəl nōt⁄bŏok] **76** 15

split [splĭt] **10** 17

split end [splĭt⁄ ĕnd⁄] **93** 6

spoke [spōk] **52** 26

sponge [spŭnj] **34** 7

(sponge) mop [spŭnj⁄ mŏp⁄] **35** 6

(spool of) thread [spōōl⁄ əv thrĕd⁄] **101** 2

spoon [spōōn] **29** 8

sports car [spörts⁄ kär⁄] **53** 17

sports [spörts] **92–97**

spotlight [spŏt⁄līt⁄] **99** 4

sprain [sprān] **40** 13

spray can [sprā⁄ kăn⁄] **12** 24

spray starch [sprā⁄ stärch⁄] **35** 21

spread [sprĕd] **17** 11

Spring [sprĭng] **26**

sprinkler [sprĭng⁄klər] **27** 13, **87** 14

sprocket [sprŏk⁄ət] **52** 20

square [skwër] **79** 9

squid [skwĭd] **62** 5

squirrel [skwür⁄əl] **66** 10

stage [stāj] **99** 5

staircase [stër⁄kās⁄] **28** 12

stake [stāk] **88** 30

stamp [stămp] **46** 10

stands [stăndz] **93** 10

staple remover [stăp⁄əl rə mōō⁄vər] **83** 29

stapler [stăp⁄lər] **83** 27

star [stär] **74** 4

starfish [stär⁄fĭsh⁄] **62** 7

starting gate [stär⁄tĭng gāt⁄] **95** 20

station [stā⁄shən] **54** 18

station wagon [stā⁄shən wăg⁄ən] **50**

steak [stāk] **10** 5, **10** 29, **18** 21

steam [stēm] **31** 12

steamer [stēm⁄ər] **30** 3

steering wheel [stïr⁄ĭng wēl⁄] **50** 8

stem [stĕm] **8** 2a, **60** 1a

step [stĕp] **28** 13

stepladder [stĕp⁄lăd⁄ər] **35** 1

stereo cassette player [stĕr⁄ē ō kə sĕt⁄ plā⁄ər] **100** 25

stereo system [stĕr⁄ē ō sĭs⁄təm] **28** 20

stern [stürn] **58** 11

stethoscope [stĕth⁄ə skōp⁄] **39** 9

stewing meat [stōō⁄ĭng mēt⁄] **10** 4

stick [stĭk] **12** 5

stick shift [stĭk⁄ shĭft⁄] **50** 24

sting [stĭng] **63** 8a

stingray [stĭng⁄rā⁄] **65** 6

stir [stür] **31** 1

stitch [stĭch] **101** 19

stitches [stĭch⁄əz] **39** 21

stockings [stŏk⁄ĭngz] **22** 6

stomach [stŭm⁄ək] **4** 66

stomachache [stŭm⁄ək āk⁄] **40** 7

stool [stōōl] **78** 34

stopper [stŏp⁄ər] **34** 10, **78** 10

stork [störk] **64** 30

stove [stōv] **30** 20

straight line [strāt⁄ līn⁄] **79** 1

(strand of) beads [strănd⁄ əv bēdz⁄] **23** 7

strap [străp] **54** 8

straw [strö] **16** 10

strawberry [strö⁄bër⁄ē] **8** 15

strawberry shortcake [strö⁄bër ē shört⁄kāk] **18** 26

stream [strēm] **88** 6

street [strēt] **44** 31

street cleaner [strēt/ klē/nər] **49** 1
street sign [strēt/ sīn/] **44** 8
streetcar [strēt/kär/] **54** 30
streetlight [strēt/līt/] **44** 29
stretch [strĕch] **95** 19
stretch bandage [strĕch/ băn/ dĭj]
   40 14
stretcher [strĕch/ər] **39** 12
stretchie [strĕch/ē] **33** 19
string [strĭng] **46** 20, **98** 10a
string bean(s) [strĭng/ bēn(z)/] **6** 15
strings [strĭngz] **98**
striped [strīpt] **24** 17
stroller [strō/lər] **33** 14
student [stōō/dənt] **76** 19
stuffed animal [stŭft/ ăn/ə məl] **33** 27
subject [sŭb/jəkt] **47** 10
submarine [sŭb/mə rēn/] **48** 7
subway [sŭb/wā/] **54**
subway station [sŭb/wā stā/shən]
   44 16
sugar (packet) [shŏŏg/ər păk/ət] **16** 13
sugar bowl [shŏŏg/ər bōl/] **29** 23
sugarcane [shŏŏg/ər kān/] **60** 20
suitcase [sōōt/kās/] **56** 7
Summer [sŭm/ər] **26**
sun [sŭn] **74** 7, **80** 3
sunbather [sŭn/bā/dhər] **90** 19
sundae [sŭn/dē] **18** 23
sunflower [sŭn/flow/ər] **60** 19
sunglasses [sŭn/glăs/əz] **90** 14
sunny [sŭn/ē] **25** 4
(sunnyside-up) egg
   [sŭn/ē sīd ŭp/ĕg/] **18** 32
sunroof [sŭn/rōōf/] **50** 44
suntan lotion [sŭn/tăn lō/shən] **90** 39
supermarket [sōō/pər mär/kət] **14**
surf [sürf] **96** 12
surfboard [sürf/börd/] **90** 25
surgery [sür/jə rē] **41** 2
suspect [sŭs/pĕkt] **43** 3
swan [swŏn] **64** 28
sweatband [swĕt/bănd/] **20** 12
sweater [swĕt/ər] **19** 7, **19** 13, **19** 23
sweatpants [swĕt/pănts/] **20** 10
sweatshirt [swĕt/shürt/] **20** 8
sweep [swēp] **38** 7

swimmer [swĭm/ər] **90** 28
swing [swĭng] **33** 24
swings [swĭngz] **87** 16
switch [swĭch] **36** 43c
switchboard [swĭch/börd/] **83** 3
switchboard operator
   [swĭch/börd ŏp/ə rā tər] **83** 1
swordfish [sörd/fĭsh/] **65** 3
synthesizer [sĭn/thə sī/zər] **99** 21
syringe [sə rĭnj/] **39** 27
syrup [sĭr/əp] **18** 6
T-shirt [tē/shürt/] **20** 29
table [tā/bəl] **29** 7
tablecloth [tā/bəl klöth/] **29** 16
tablet [tăb/lət] **41** 6
taco [tŏ/kō] **18** 24
tadpole [tăd/pōl/] **65** 16
tail [tāl] **57** 10, **65** 3a, **66** 3a
taillight [tāl/līt/] **50** 31
tailor [tā/lər] **84** 6
take [tāk] **17** 10
takeoff [tāk/ŏf/] **57**
Takla Makan Desert
   [tŏk/lə mə kŏn/ dĕz/ərt] **70** 53
tambourine [tăm/bə rēn/] **98** 17
tank [tăngk] **48** 10
tank top [tăngk/ tŏp/] **20** 13
tanker [tăngk/ər] **58** 15
tap [tăp] **16** 20
tape [tāp] **46** 22
tape measure [tāp/ mĕzh/ ər] **36** 21,
   101 15
taxi [tăk/sē] **54**
taxi stand [tăk/sē stănd/] **54** 28
taxicab [tăk/sē kăb/] **54** 27
tea [tē] **16** 15
teacher [tē/chər] **76** 4
teakettle [tē/kĕt/əl] **30** 28
team sports [tēm/spörts/] **92**
teapot [tē/pŏt/] **29** 19
tear [tër] **77** 9
teddy bear [tĕd/ē bër/] **33** 3
tee [tē] **95** 13
telephone [tĕl/ə fōn/] **83** 15
telescope [tĕl/ə skōp/] **74** 22
television [tĕl/ə vĭzh/ən] **28** 18, **100** 5
teller [tĕl/ər] **86** 15

temperature [tĕm/pər ə chər] **25** 6
Tennessee [tĕn/ə sē/] **72** 42
tennis [tĕn/əs] **94**
tennis ball [tĕn/əs böl/] **94** 1
tennis court [tĕn/əs kört/] **95**
tent [tĕnt] **88** 24
tentacle [tĕn/tə kəl] **62** 12a
terminal [türm/ə nəl] **50** 55, **58** 29
terminal building [türm/ə nəl bĭl/dĭng]
   57 16
termite [tür/mīt] **63** 11
terrier [tër/ē ər] **68** 25
test tube [tĕst/tōōb/] **78** 9
Texas [tĕk/səs] **72** 43
textbook [tĕkst/bŏŏk/] **76** 26
theater [thē/ə tər] **99**
thermometer
   [thər mŏm/ə tər] **25** 5, **78** 22
thermos [thür/məs] **88** 14
thigh [thī] **4** 18, **10** 19
thimble [thĭm/bəl] **101** 21
third (1/3) [thürd] **79** 32
third baseman [thürd/ bās/mən] **93** 4
thorn [thörn] **60** 18c
thread [thrĕd] **36** 42b, **101** 2
three-piece suit [thrē/pēs sōōt/] **20** 40
throat [thrōt] **4** 59
through [thrōō] **103** 1
throw [thrō] **96** 10
thumb [thŭm] **4** 24
thumbtack [thŭm/tăk/] **76** 25
ticket [tĭk/ət] **54** 16, **56** 4
ticket window [tĭk/ət wĭn/dō] **54** 19
tie (n) [tī] **20** 47
tie (v) [tī] **77** 12
tie clip [tī/ klĭp/] **23** 14
tie pin [tī/ pĭn/] **23** 13
tiger [tī/gər] **68** 2
tight [tīt] **24** 3
tighten [tī/tən] **38** 4
tight end [tīt/ ĕnd/] **93** 30
tights [tīts] **19** 14
tile [tīl] **34** 27
timer [tī/mər] **78** 13
timetable [tīm/tā/bəl] **54** 20

tip [tĭp] **54** 22

tire [tīr] **50** 37, **52** 28

tissues [tĭsh/o͞oz] **32** 13

title [tī/təl] **47** 9

to [to͞o] **103** 9

toast [tōst] **18** 34

toaster [tōs/tər] **30** 16

toe [tō] **4** 54

toenail [tō/nāl/] **4** 56

toilet [toy/lət] **34** 29

toilet brush [toy/lət brŭsh/] **34** 31

toilet paper [toy/lət pā/pər] **34** 30

toiletries [toy/lə trēz] **23**

token booth [tō/kən bo͞oth/] **54** 13

tollbooth [tōl/bo͞oth/] **53** 27

tomato(es) [tə mā/tō(z)] **7** 19

tongs [tŏngz] **78** 29

tongue [tŭng] **4** 41

tongue depressor [tŭng/ də prĕs/ər] **40** 12

toolbox [to͞ol/bŏks/] **36** 23

toolshed [to͞ol/shĕd/] **27** 28

tooth [to͞oth] **4** 42

toothache [to͞oth/āk/] **40** 9

toothbrush [to͞oth/brŭsh/] **34** 21

toothless mammals [to͞oth/ləs măm/əlz] **66**

toothpaste [to͞oth/pāst/] **34** 16

tortoise [tör/təs] **65** 18

tossed salad [töst/ săl/əd] **18** 13

touch [tŭch] **77** 2

touring handlebars [to͝or/ĭng hăn/dəl bärz] **52** 12

tow truck [tō/trŭk] **49** 2

toward [törd] **103** 4

towel rack [tow/əl răk/] **34** 25

towrope [tō/rōp/] **59** 11

toy chest [toy/chĕst/] **33** 29

track [trăk] **54** 10, **94** 32

track and field [trăk/ənd fēld/] **94**

tractor [trăk/tər] **81** 15

tractor trailer [trăk/tər trā/lər] **49** 15

traffic cop [trăf/ək kŏp/] **44** 10

traffic light [trăf/ək līt/] **44** 21

trailer [trā/lər] **53** 10

train [trān] **54**

training wheels [trān/ĭng wēlz/] **52** 1

transcript [trăn/skrĭpt] **43** 15

transfer [trăns/fər] **54** 4

transformer [trăns för/mər] **80** 25

transmission towers [trănz mĭsh/ən tow/ərz] **80** 23

transportation [trăns/pər tā/shən] **54**

transporter [trăns/ pör tər] **49** 17

trash basket [trăsh/ băs/kət] **44** 15

trash can [trăsh/ kăn/] **87** 11

travel agent [trăv/əl ā/jənt] **84** 4

traveler [trăv/ə lər] **56** 3

tray [trā] **16** 33

tray table [trā/ tā/bəl] **56** 22

treatments [trēt/mənts] **41**

tree [trē] **60** 35

trees [trēz] **60**

triangle [trī/ăng/gəl] **79** 6

tricycle [trī/sĭ kəl] **52** 6

trigger [trĭg/ər] **48** 22

tripod [trī/pŏd] **100** 9

trim [trĭm] **26** 8

trombone [trŏm bōn/] **98** 23

trough [tröf] **81** 25

trout [trowt] **65** 2

trowel [trow/əl] **27** 27

truck [trŭk] **49, 53** 25

truck driver [trŭk/ drī/vər] **49** 15

trumpet [trŭm/pət] **98** 25

trunk [trŭngk] **50** 40, **60** 35b, **66** 17a

tub [tŭb] **12** 6

tuba [to͞o/bə] **98** 27

tube [to͞ob] **12** 15, **90** 29

tugboat [tŭg/bōt/] **58** 13

tulip [to͞o/ləp] **60** 1

turkey [tür/kē] **10** 23, **64** 20

turnip [tür/nəp] **7** 34

turn signal lever [türn/ sĭg nəl lĕ/vər] **50** 11

turn signal lights [türn/ sĭg nəl līts/] **50** 50

turnstile [türn/stīl/] **54** 12

turntable [türn/tā/bəl] **100** 18

turtle [tür/təl] **65** 12

(turtleneck) sweater [tür/təl nĕk swĕ/tər] **19** 13

tusk [tŭsk] **66** 17b

TV antenna [tē/vē ăn tĕn/ə] **27** 3

tweezers [twē/zərz] **78** 32

twig [twĭg] **60** 33a

(two-door) sedan [to͞o/dör sə dăn/] **50**

type [tīp] **77** 10

typewriter [tīp/rī/tər] **83** 10

typing chair [tī/pĭng chër/] **83** 17

typist [tī/pəst] **83** 6

U.S. mailbox [yo͞o/ĕs māl/bŏks] **46** 6

U.S. Postal System [yo͞o/ĕs pōs/təl sĭs təm] **46**

ukulele [yo͞o/kə lā/lē] **98** 3

umbrella [ŭm brĕl/ə] **20** 24

umpire [ŭm/pīr] **92** 1, **93** 17

uncle [ŭng/kəl] **3** 3

under [ŭn/dər] **102** 8

underpants [ŭn/dər pănts/] **22** 3

undershirt [ŭn/dər shürt/] **22** 1

underwear [ŭn/dər wër/] **22**

uniform [yo͞o/nə förm/] **20** 45, **92** 9

United States of America [yo͞o nī/təd stāts/ əv ə mër/ə kə] **72**

universe [yo͞o/nə vürs/] **74**

up [ŭp] **103** 11

upper arm [ŭp/ər ärm/] **4** 7

Urals [yo͝or/əlz] **70** 46

uranium rods [yo͝o rā/nē əm rŏdz/] **80** 15

Uranus [yo͝or/ə nəs] **74** 17

usher [ŭsh/ər] **99** 16

Utah [yo͞o/tö] **72** 44

utility pole [yo͞o tĭl/ə tē pōl/] **80** 26

utility room [yo͞o tĭl/ə tē ro͞om/] **35**

(V-neck) sweater [vē/nĕk swĕt/ər] **19** 23

vacuum [văk/yo͞om] **38** 14

vacuum cleaner [văk/yo͞om klē/nər] **35** 16

valve [vălv] **52** 27

van [văn] **53** 26

vase [vās] **28** 6

VCR (videocassette recorder) [vē/sē är/]/ [vĭd/ē ō kə sĕt/ rə kör/dər] **100** 4

vegetables [vĕj/tə bəlz] **6**

vehicles and equipment [vē/ə kəlz ənd ə kwĭp/mənt] **48**

vein [vān] **4** 68

vendor [vĕn/dər] **87** 3

vent [vĕnt] **50** 21
Venus [vē′nəs] **74** 12
verbs [vürbz] **17, 26, 31, 38, 77, 96**
Vermont [vür mŏnt′] **72** 45
vest [vĕst] **20** 39
video [vĭd′ē ō] **100**
video camera [vĭd′ē ō kăm′ə rə] **100** 1
videocassette (tape)
  [vĭd′ē ō kə sĕt′tāp′] **100** 3
vine [vīn] **60** 42
viola [vē ōl′ə] **98** 8
violet [vī′ə lət] **60** 16
violin [vī ə lĭn′] **98** 7
Virginia [vər jĭn′yə] **72** 46
vise [vīs] **36** 36
visor [vĭz′ər] **50** 5
volleyball [vŏl′ē böl′] **92, 92** 22
waders [wā′dərz] **88** 10
waist [wāst] **4** 13
waiter [wā′tər] **16** 5
waitress [wā′trəs] **16** 2
walk [wök] **77** 8
walker [wök′ər] **33** 23
wall [wöl] **28** 3
wall unit [wöl′ yoo′nət] **28** 19
wall-to-wall carpeting
  [wöl′tə wöl kär′pə tĭng] **28** 15
wallet [wöl′ət] **20** 9
walnut(s) [wöl′nət(s)] **9** 29
walrus [wöl′rŭs] **68** 11
warm [wörm] **25** 8
wash [wŏsh] **38** 16
washcloth [wŏsh′klöth′] **34** 22
washer [wŏsh′ər] **36** 40
washing machine
  [wŏsh′ĭng mə shēn′] **35** 30
Washington [wŏsh′ĭng tən] **72** 47
wasp [wŏsp] **63** 20
wastepaper basket
  [wāst′pā pər băs′kət] **34** 13
watch [wŏch] **23** 10
watchband [wŏch′bănd′] **23** 11
water (n) [wŏt′ər] **42** 16, **90** 30
water (v) [wŏt′ər] **26** 5
water fountain [wŏt′ər fown′tən]
  87 19
water glass [wŏt′ər glăs′] **29** 6

waterfall [wŏt′ər föl′] **80** 11, **88** 18
water-skier [wŏt′ər skē′ər] **59** 10
watercress [wŏt′ər krĕs′] **6** 5
watering can [wŏt′ər ĭng kăn′] **27** 16
watermelon [wŏt′ər mĕl′ən] **8** 26
wave [wāv] **90** 24
weapons [wĕp′ənz] **48**
weather [wĕdh′ər] **25**
weather forecaster
  [wĕdh′ər för′kăst ər] **86** 1
weather satellite [wĕdh′ər săt′ə līt]
  75 3
weaving [wē′vĭng] **101** 30
web [wĕb] **63** 15
wedding ring [wĕd′ĭng rĭng′] **23** 4
weights [wāts] **78** 5
west [wĕst] **70** 74
West Virginia [wĕst′vər jĭn′yə] **72** 48
wet [wĕt] **25** 15
wet suit [wĕt′soot′] **90** 38
whale [wāl] **68** 9
wheat [wēt] **60** 22
wheat farm [wēt′ färm′] **81**
(wheat) field [wēt′ fēld′] **81** 16
wheel [wēl] **52** 4
wheelbarrow [wēl′băr′ō] **27** 32,
  82 23
wheelchair [wēl′chër′] **39** 2
whistle [wĭs′əl] **90** 5
whole [hōl] **10** 27, **79** 29
whole (chicken) [hōl′ chĭk′ən] **10** 16
width [wĭdth] **79** 35
wife [wīf] **2** 4
willow [wĭl′ō] **60** 31
wind [wĭnd] **80** 4
windbreaker [wĭnd′brā′kər] **19** 5
windlass [wĭnd′ləs] **58** 23
windmill [wĭnd′mĭl′] **80** 19
window [wĭn′dō] **27** 7, **46** 15
window cleaner [wĭn′dō klē′nər]
  35 10
windpipe [wĭnd′pīp′] **4** 60
windshield [wĭnd′shēld′] **50** 45
windshield wiper [wĭnd′shēld wī′pər]
  50 6
windsurfer [wĭnd′sür′fər] **59** 14
windy [wĭn′dē] **25** 13

wine [wīn] **16** 19
wine glass [wīn′ glăs′] **29** 5
wing [wĭng] **10** 22, **57** 9, **63** 4a, **64** 1a
Winter [wĭn′tər] **26**
wipe [wīp] **38** 5
wire [wīr] **36** 35
wire mesh screen [wīr′ mĕsh skrēn′]
  78 6
Wisconsin [wĭs kŏn′sən] **72** 49
witness [wĭt′nəs] **43** 13
witness stand [wĭt′nəs stănd′] **43** 18
wolf [woolf] **68** 29
woman [woom′ən] **2** 1
wood [wood] **36** 4
wood plane [wood′ plān′] **36** 32
woodpecker [wood′pĕk′ər] **64** 17
woods [woodz] **88** 32
woodwinds [wood′wĭndz′] **98**
wool [wool] **101** 23
word processor [würd′ prŏ′sĕs ər]
  83 7
work gloves [würk′ glŭvz′] **27** 26
workbench [würk′bĕnch′] **36** 22
workshop [würk′shŏp′] **36**
world [würld] **70**
worm [würm] **62** 11
wrench [rĕnch] **36** 10
wrist [rĭst] **4** 21
write [rīt] **77** 7
writer [rī′tər] **86** 7
Wyoming [wī ō′mĭng] **72** 50
X ray [ĕks′ rā′] **39** 1
X ray screener [ĕks′rā skrē′nər] **56** 11
xylophone [zī′lə fōn′] **98** 31
yam [yăm] **6** 24
Yangtze River [yăng′sē rĭv′ər] **70** 69
yarn [yärn] **101** 31
Yellow Sea [yĕl′ō sē′] **70** 37
Yenisey River [yĕn′ə sā′ rĭv′ər] **70** 65
Yukon River [yoo′kŏn rĭv′ər] **70** 56
zebra [zē′brə] **66** 18
zinnia [zĭn′ē ə] **60** 13
zip code [zĭp′kōd′] **46** 12
zipper [zĭp′ər] **101** 16
zoo [zoo] **87** 1
zucchini [zoo kē′nē] **6** 27

가금류 **11** B
가는 눈금있는 판 **78** 14
가로등 **45** 29
가로장 **82** 9
가리비 **11** 35, **62** 10
가르마 **14** 31
까마귀 **64** 3
가벼운 질병 및 상처 **40**
가사와 관련된 업무 **85** B
가속장치 **50** 27
가솔린 펌프 **53** 14
가수 **99** 24
가스 게이지 **50** 9
가스탱크 **50** 34
가슴 **4** 12, **11** 21
가시 **60** 18, **66** 11
가오리 **65** 6
가운뎃 손가락 **4** 26
가위 **101** 17
가을 **26**
가정용품 **15** 15
가제패드 **39** 25
가져가다 **17** 10
가족 **3**
가족용 식당 **16** A
가족용 식당과 칵테일 라운지 **16**
가지 **17** 21, **61** 35
가축 **81** 12, **81** 20
가축 우리 **81** 24
가터벨트 **22** 14
각뿔 **79** 25
깎아 다듬다 **26** 8
깍지 강남콩 **6** 15
간 **5** 65
간고기 **10** 2
간단한 동물 **62**
간식 **15** 18
간이 음식점 **90** 2
간이차 **80** 8
간지스 강 **71** 67
간편화 **21** 42
간헐천 **80** 5
간호원 **39** 19
깔때기 **78** 17
긁는 동물 **66**
갈고리 및 눈 **101** 14
갈매기 **64** 4
갈비 **10** 10
갈아입히기용 책상 **33** 9
갈아타는 표 **54** 4
갈아 끼우다 **38** 13
갈음용 걸레 **35** 11
갈퀴 **27** 30, **81** 14
감기 **40** 11
감로멜론 **9** 35
감염 **40** 14
감옥 **43** 1
감자 **7** 23
감자깡 **18** 4

감자 튀김 **18** 28
갑판 **58** 22
갓난아기 방 **33**
갓난아기용 위 아래가 딸린 옷 **33** 19
갓난아기의 놀이터 **33** 30
강 **71**
강남콩 **6** 13
강아지 **69** 27
깡통 **12** 10
깡통 따개 **30**
개 **69**
개구리 **65** 17
깨끗한 **24** 6
깨다 **31** 7
개똥벌레 **63** 17
개미 **63** 13
개미 핥기 **66** 5
개암 **9** 30
개울 **88** 6
개인 스포츠 **94**
개인용 콤퓨터 **100** 31
개인전용 비행기 **57** 3
개폐식 천장달린 지붕 **51** 44
색실 **56** 19
거들 **22** 15
거리 **45** 31
거리 청소차 **49** 1
거미 **63** 16
거미줄 **63** 15
거북 **65** 18
거실 **28**
거울 **32** 5
거울달린 옷장 **32** 9
거위 **64** 26
(물을)건너서 **103** 6
건물 번호 **45** 24
건반 **98** 1a
건반악기 연주자 **99** 22
건설공사 인부 **82** 14
건조기계 **35** 24
건조한 **25** 14
건초 **81** 13
건축가 **86** 8
건축공사 **82**
건축공사장 **82** A
건축업자 **82** 5
건포도 **9** 24
걷다 **77** 8
걸다 **38** 6
걸레 **35** 4
걸쇠 **23** 17, **32** 1
걸이 **36** 16, **78** 8
검은색 **104**
검찰관 **43** 17
검은 딸기 **8** 12
껍질 **9** 20, **9** 37, **62** 1a
껍질을 벗기다 **31** 5
게 **11** 36, **62** 9
게시판 **76** 7

겨드랑이 **4** 10
겨울 **26**
겨자 **18** 1
격납고 **57** 17
격자 무늬의 **24** 22
견과류 **9**
견본 **101** 6
견인차 **49** 2
견인 트레일러 **49** 15
결승선 **95** 21
결재 서류함 **83** 12
결혼반지 **23** 4
겹자 모양의 퍼센트 **78** 28
경마의 기수 **94** 21
경마장 **95** D
경비원 **56** 9, **86** 14
경적 **50** 12, **52** 5
경주로 **94** 32
경찰관 **43** 6
경찰서 **43** A
계기 **56** 14
계기판 **50** 19
계단난간 **28** 12
계류장치 **59** 19
계산기 **15** 21, **83** 19
계산대 **15** 21
계산서 **16** 14
계산하다 **17** 7
계선장 **58** 28
계선주 **58** 26
계심봉 **51** 58
계절에 관한 동사 **26**
고구마 **7** 24
고기 가금 및 해물류 **10** 11
고기굽는 기구 **30** 33
고기 따위를 가르다 **31** 6
고기류 **10** A
고기 붙은 돼지 갈비 **18** 15
고기와 양상치가 든 옥수수 빵 **18** 24
고기완자 **18** 11
고래 **68** 9
꼬리 **57** 10, **65** 3a
고릴라 **69** 17
고르덴 바지 **21** 27
고무관 **78** 18
고무 보오트 **89** 16
고무 보오트 놀이 **89**
고무 젖꼭지 **33** 22
고비사막 **71** 54
고삐 **94** 22
고속도로 여행 **53**
고양이 **68** 4
고원 **88** 1
고정나사 **37** 39
고추 **7** 22
고치 **63** 2
고혈압 **40** 10
곡괭이 **82** 13
꼭 껜 **24** 3

곡선 **79** 3
꼭지 **8** 2, **16** 20
곤충 **63**
곤충물림 **40** 3
골그물 **92** 20
골대 **93** 35
골무 **101** 21
골문 **92** 35
골반 **4** 16
골프 **94**
골프공 **94** 7
골프백 **95** 7
골프장 밖의 잡초가 우거진 곳 **95** 6
골프 채 **94** 9, **95** 5
골프치는 사람 **94** 10
골프 카트 **95** 8
골프 코스 **95** B
곰 **69**
공격 끝선 **93** 30
공공 도서관 **47**
공공 운송기관 **55**
공군 **48** 19
공기 여과기 **51** 52
공기 펌프 **53** 13
공원 **85** 12
공원 순찰대 **88** 5
공작새 **64** 18
공장일 **85** C
공중선 **51** 46
공중전화 **44** 7
공중 케이블 카 **55** 31
공항 체크인 **56**
꽃 **60**
꽃상치 **6** 7
꽃잎 **60** 18
꽈리 **8** 11
과수 **81** 2
과수원 **81** 1
과일류 **8, 9**
과자 **18** 22
과학 실험실 **78**
관람석 **93** 10
관상대원 **86** 1
관제탑 **57** 20
관현악단 **99** 6
괄태충 **62** 4
교과서 **76** 26
교사 **76** 4
교실 **76**
교통 경찰관 **44** 10
교통 신호등 **45** 21
교환대 **83** 3
교환수 **83** 1
구강 위생기사 **39** 14
구근 **60** 8a
구급차 **42** 6
구기 시합장 **93**
구두 **21** 49
구두끈 **20** 7

구두뒷굽 **20** 5
구두밑창 **20** 6
구렛나루 **4** 39
구름이 낀 **25** 2
구멍 **94** 8
구멍뚫림용 귀걸이 **23** 16
구명구 **90** 9
구명복 **59** 1
구명정 **90** 10
구운빵 **18** 34
구운 제품 **14** 11
구워낸 콩 **18** 3
구월 **104**
구유(여물통) **81** 25
구조선 **58** 19
구조원 **90** 6
구조원용 의자 **90** 8
구차(공을려 놓는 자리) **95** 13
구차와 그린 사이의 **95** 12
국기 **76** 1
국화 **60** 4
군감자 **18** 20
군대(육 해 공군) **48**
군인 **48** 16
굴 **11** 33, **62** 2
굴뚝 **29** 9, **58** 18, **80** 22
굽는 팬 **30** 17
굽달린 큰 컵 **78** 23
굽이 높은 구두 **20** 25
권총 **43** 7
권총용 가죽지갑 **43** 8
권투 **94**
권투장 **94** 17
꿩 **64** 19
궤도 **54** 10, **74** 21
귀 **4** 34
귀걸이 **23** 1
귀걸이 끼우개 **23** 15
귀뚜라미 **63** 5
귀리 **60** 23
귀마개 **19** 10
귤 **8** 8
귤껍질 **8** 8
귤조각 **8** 8
그네 **33** 25, **87** 16
끄는 밧줄 **59** 11
그릇 **12** 2
그리다 **77** 11
그림 **28** 5
그림 맞추기 **33** 31
그레이트 샌디 사막 **71** 55
그레이프후루트 **8** 7
그물 **88** 9
그을음 방지용 세제 **91** 39
근대 **7** 33
근육 **5** 62
(등대) 근처에(서) **103** 2
글라이더 **57** 4
글러브 **94** 11, **94** 15

긁어벗기다 **26** 15
긁어모으다 **26** 10
끓이다 **31** 16
금관악기 **98**
금성 **74** 12
금속용 쇠톱 **36** 18
금속 탐지기 **56** 10
금요일 **104**
금잔화속의 식물 **60** 6
급류 **89** 17
기 **82** 20, **95** 9
기관사 **55** 15
기관총 **48** 25
기구 **39** 13
기니아만 **70** 25
기름을 치다 **38** 12
기린 **67** 29
기상 위성 **75** 3
기어 변속기 **52** 22
기어 변환 레버 **50** 24
기자 **86** 11
기중기 **58** 6
기초 **82** 11
기체 **57** 14
기타 **98** 11
기타 단장 **99** 25
기타 수공예 **101** B
기타 식물 **61**
기타 악기류 **98**
기타 운송기관 **55** E
기하학적 도형 **79** B
긴 **24** 2
긴 소매 **20** 15
긴 의자 **44** 14, **87** 10
긴팔 원숭이 **69** 15
긴호박 **7** 27
길모퉁이 **44** 3
길이 **79** 36
깁스 붕대 **39** 5
깃털 **64** 7a
깊은 남비 **30** 13
깊이 **79** 33
나르다 **26** 16
나무 **61** 35
나무(판자) **36** 4
나무껍질 **61** 35
나무딸기 **8** 16
나무메 **36** 11
나방 **63** 21
나비 **63** 3
나사 **37** 42
나사돌리개 **37** 24
나사머리 **37** 42
나사못 **37** 38
나사산 **37** 42
나선형 노트 **76** 15
나이프 **29** 15
나일강 **71** 63
나팔수선화 **60** 8

낙농장 **81** A
낚시질 **88**
낚싯대 **88** 7
낚싯줄 **88** 8
낙타 **67** 33
낙하산 **48** 6
난간동자 **28** 11
난초 **60** 12
날 **37** 43
날개 **11** 22, **57** 9, **63** 4a, **64** 1a
낡은 **24** 14
날씨를 설명하는데 쓰이는 말 **25**
남극 **70** 7
남극해 **70** 14
남대서양 **70** 12
남미 **70** 2
남비집게 **30** 34
남(배)우 **99** 19
남성용 수영 팬츠 **91** 33
남성용 잠옷 **22** 19
남자 **2** 2
남자목동 **81** 21
남종업원 **16** 5
남쪽 **71** 72
남지나해 **70** 39
남편 **2** 3, **3** 12
남태평양 **70** 10
남학생용 중앙 버팀쇠 **52** 11
낮은 **24** 12
내의 **22** 7
내장기관 **5** F
냅킨 **29** 14
냉각탑 **80** 16
냉동식품 **14** 2
냉동실 **14** 3, **30** 20
냉방장치 **32** 11
냉장고 **30** 19
넘어지다 **96** 7
넙치류 **65** 7
네거리 **44** 11
네모나사 돌리개 **37** 25
네바다 **73** 28
네브라스카 **73** 27
네줄 소형 기타 **98** 3
네트 **92** 23, **95** 2
넥타이 **21** 47
넥타이 클립 **23** 14
넥타이핀 **23** 13
넷 **104**
노 **59** 3, **59** 22
노란색 **104**
노로 젓는 배 **59** 23
노받이 **59** 21
노쓰다코타 **73** 34
노쓰캐롤리나 **73** 33
녹색 **104**
놀이터 **87** 15
농구 **92**
농구공 **92** 21

농부 **81** 7
농업 및 목축 **81**
농장안의 주택 **81** 3
높은 **24** 11
높이 **79** 34
뇌 **5** 57
누 (베이스) **92** 6
누빔 **101** 32
누임용 침대 **39** 12
누워 요양하기 **41** 1
눈 **5** D
눈꺼풀 **5** 45
눈금이 새겨진 유리 원기통 **78** 25
눈동자(동공) **5** 48
눈썹 **5** 44
눈썹 연필 **23** 26
눈이 오는 **25** 3
눈 치우다 **26** 13
눌림 쇠 **101** 13
뉴멕시코 **73** 31
뉴스 방송 해설자 **86** 2
뉴욕 **73** 32
뉴저어지 **73** 30
뉴햄프셔 **73** 29
느릅나무 **61** 36
느슨한 바지 **30** 4
늑대 **69** 29
니나 강 **71** 66
니제르 강 **71** 61
다갈색 **104**
따다 **26** 7
따뜻한 **25** 8
다람쥐 **66** 10
다리 **4** 17, **11** 14, 20
다리미 **35** 12
다리미질 하다 **38** 11
다림질 판 **35** 13
다섯(오) **104**
다용도실 **35**
다이브하다 **97** 14
딱다구리 **64** 17
딱정벌레 **63** 10
닦아내다 **38** 5, **38** 9
단궤철도 **55** 29
단추 **20** 3, **101** 9
단추구멍 **101** 8
단체 운동 경기 **92**
단층식 주택(지붕의 경사가 완만한) **27** A
단풍나무 **61** 38
닫다 **77** 5
닫힌 **24** 16
달 **74** 9
딸 **3** 15
달걀말이 튀김 **18** 25
달걀후라이 **18** 32
딸기 **8** 15
딸기류 **8**
딸기케이크 **18** 26
딸랑이 **33** 21

달력 **83** 9
달리는 사람 **91** 23
달리다 **96** 6
달의 위상 **74** C
달 착륙 **75** B
달 착륙선 **75** 7
달팽이 **62** 1
담배 **16** 31
담뱃대 **16** 26
담요 **32** 20
당근 **7** 32
당나귀 **67** 23
땅콩 **9** 28
닻 **58** 24
닻줄통 **58** 23
닭 **64** 23
닭고기 **11** 24
대 **37** 43
대각선 **79** 20
대기권의 **74** A
대륙 **70**
때밀이 수건 **34** 22
대양 **70**
대추 **9** 23
대포 **48** 11
대패 **37** 32
대합 **11** 32
댐 **80** 18
떠나다 **77** 13
더듬이 **62** 1b
더운물 수도꼭지 **34** 17
던지다 **97** 10
덤프 트럭 **49** 14
덧문 **27** 8
덩굴 **61** 42
덩어리 숯 **27** 23
덩굴 옻나무(아이비) **61** 45
덩굴 옻나무(오크) **61** 43
덩굴월귤 **8** 13
덮개 **28** 7
데이지 **60** 5
델라웨어 **72** 8
도끼 **42** 14
도로가 **45** 26
도로공사 **82** B
도로와 땅의 연결부 **53** 22
도로표지 **44** 8, **53** 23
도마 **30** 26
도마뱀 **65** 15
도보여행자 **88** 2
도보용 반장화 **19** 9
도살업자 **84** 13
도서관 증 **47** 3
도시 **44**, **45** 21
도시락 통 **21** 31
도안 **101** 7
도자기 **29** 1
도토리 **61** 33
도토리 호박 **61** 28

도표 종이 **78** 11
독수리 **64** 5
돌고래 **68** 13
동네 공원 **87**
동력 생성 장치 **80** B
동력자원 **80** A
동맥 **5** 69
동물 노리개 **33** 27
동물원 **87** 1
동전 **13** 26
동쪽 **71** 73
동지나해 **70** 38
돛 **59** 9
돛대 **59** 8
돛단배 **59** 4
돛의 아래 활대 **59** 7
뜨리쇠 **37** 40
돼지 **67** 30
돼지고기 **10** 6
돼지불고기 **10** 8
두건달린 모피옷 **19** 8
두껍고 헐거운 스웨터 **20** 8
두껍게 베어낸 돼지고깃점 **10** 9
뚜껑 **30** 9
뚜껑있는 찜남비 **30** 14
두통 **40** 6
둔각 **79** 5
둘(이) **104**
둘레 난간이 있는(소아용의) 침대 **33** 4
둥그런 빵 **18** 7
둥근 고무관 **91** 29
둥근달 **74** 24
둥근 몸통 **50** 13
둥근 톱 **36** 20
둥우리 **64** 31
뛰다 **96** 8
뒤뜰 **27** C
뒤밤바 **51** 42
(의자)뒤에 (서) **102** 9
뒷다리 **66** 3
뒷받침 살 **52** 9
뒷좌석 **50** 32
뜨개바늘 **101** 25
뜨개질 **101** 22
뜨거운 **25** 7
드레싱친 샐러드 **18** 13
득점판 **93** 19
듣다 **77** 6
들다 **17** 12
들다람쥐 **66** 8
들소 **67** 19
들어가다 **77** 14
등 **4** 11
등대 **58** 14
등딱지 **65** 18
등산 **89**
등산용 멜빵 **89** 22
등없는 걸상 **78** 34
등짐기구 **89** 28

등짐용 가방 **19** 4
디스크 자키 **86** 9
디젤 연료 **80** 34
라디에이터 **51** 56
라디오 **50** 18
라이터 **16** 30
라임 **8** 10
라케트 **94** 2, **94** 18, **94** 29
라케트 공 **94** 29
라케트 경기 **94** 18
라크로스(하키 비슷한 구기의 일종) **92**
라크로스 스틱 **92** 16
랍테브해 **70** 33
랜턴 **89** 29
러브알칼리 사막 **71** 52
레몬 **8** 9
레이블 **46** 21
레인 **94** 4
레인 양쪽에 홈 **94** 3
레코드 **100** 23
렌즈 **100** 6
렌치 **36** 10
로드아일랜드 **73** 39
로비 **44** 2
로케트 **75** 13
록 그룹 **99** C
록키 산맥 **71** 40
롤러 **37** 29
롤러팬 **37** 28
롤빵 **18** 19
루스리프식 종이 **76** 13
루이지아나 **72** 18
루터(철 나무를 짜르는 대패의 일종) **37** 37
리마콩 **6** 16
리오그랜데 강 **71** 57
링 스텐드 **78** 19
마개 **16** 18, **34** 10, **78** 10
마개뽑이 **16** 17
마늘 **7** 25
마늘쪽 **7** 25
마른 과일류 **9**
마시다 **17** 2
마스카라 **23** 28
마이크로 필림 **47** 13
마이크로 필림 판독기 **4** 14
마차 **55** 33
마흔(사십) **104**
막대기 모양의 물건 **12** 5
만도린 **98** 4
만지다 **77** 2
말 **67** 21, **81** 23
말뚝 **89** 30
말린자두 **9** 22
말채나무 **61** 28
말타기 **94**
말타는 사람 **87** 6
망과 **8** 5
망아지 **67** 22
망원경 **74** 22

망치 **36** 13
매 **6** 47
매릴랜드 **72** 20
매샤추서츠 **72** 21
매스콤 및 기술 **86** A
매트 **50** 22
매표소 **55** 19
매형 매제 **3** 11
맥주 **16** 23
미등 **50** 31
머리 **4** 20, **4** 36
머리띠 **20** 12
머리말리는 기계 **34** 26
머리받침 **50** 35
머리 보호장치 **94** 14
머리솔 **32** 7
머리카락 **4** 30
머리털 **67** 21
먹다 **17** 1
먼지를 털다 **38** 15
먼지털이 **35** 2
멈춤용 시계 **78** 13
멍든 눈 **40** 5
멍키렌치 **36** 12
면도기 **23** 20
면도용 크림 **23** 22
면도칼 **23** 23
면도후 바르는 로숀 **23** 21
면샤쓰 **19** 3
면양 **67** 25
명왕성 **74** 19
메니퀴어용 에나멜 **23** 25
메뚜기 **63** 6
메리 스미스씨의 가족 **3**
메리야스 **22** 1
메인 **72** 19
멕시코만 **70** 19
멜빵고리 **89** 27
모기 **63** 13
모니터 **100** 32
모닥불 **89** 31
모델 **86** 5
모래 **91** 31
모래구덩이 **95** 11
모래놀이통 **87** 13
모래를 뿌리다 **25** 14
모래삽 **90** 17
모래성 **91** 32
모래언덕 **90** 12
모자 **19** 2, **19** 18, **21** 43, **92** 11
모자보 사막 **71** 48
모충 **63** 1
모델 **90** 3
모판 벼 **60** 21
목 **4** 4
목걸이 **23** 6
목공 **85** 2
목관악기 **98**
목구멍 **5** 59

목도리 **19** 19
목련 **61** 29
목발 **39** 7
목성 **74** 15
목스웨터 **19** 7
목요일 **104**
목욕용 실내복 **22** 20
목이 아픔 **40** 12
목장 **81** 6
목화 스왑 **33** 10
몬타나 **73** 26
몸전체를 닦는 큰 수건 **34** 24
몹시 추운 **25** 11
못 **37** 41
못바늘 **23** 8
무기 및 탄약 **48** C
무게 추 **78** 5
무늬를 날염한 **24** 21
무당벌레 **63** 14
무대 **99** 5
무대장면 **99** 2
무릎 **4** 19
무릎 양말 **22** 16
무용수 **99** 3
무화과 **9** 21
묶다 **77** 12
문 손잡이 **50** 4
문어 **62** 6
문지기 **92** 24
문지르는 도구 **36** 14
문지르다 **38** 2
문질러 잘게 썰다 **31** 2
물 **4** 216
물갈퀴 **68** 12
물고기 **65** A
물고기 및 파충류 **65**
물뿌리개 **27** 13, **87** 14
물에서 사는 포유동물 **68**
물엿 **18** 6
물잔 **29** 6
물주다 **26** 5
물주전자 **29** 4
물통 **39** 16
미국 너구리 **77** 12
미국 삼나무 **61** 25
미국 우체통 **46** 6
미국 우편국 제도 **46**
미끄럼틀 **87** 12
미나리 **6** 5
미나리아재비 **60** 17
미네소타 **72** 23
미등 **50** 31
미시간 **72** 22
미시시피 **72** 24
미시피 강 **71** 58
미 축구 **92**
미 축구공 **92** 13
미 축구용 안전모 **92** 14
미 축구장 **93** B

미 용사 **84** 10
미 조리 **73** 25
미 터 **55** 23
미 합중국의 주명칭 **72, 73**
밀 **60** 22
밀 농장 **81** B
밀 다 **26** 12
밀 방망이 **30** 25
밀밭 **81** 16
밀어올리는 기계 **51** 38
밑변 **79** 7
(언덕)밑에(서) **102** 8
(책상)밑에(서) **103** 3
바께쓰 **35** 19, **90** 16
바구나 **34** 28
바나나 **9** 20
바늘 **101** 18
바늘꽂이 **101** 3
바늘끝 **101** 26
바늘뜸 **101** 19
바다거북 **65** 12
바다와 만 **70**
바다표범 **68** 12
바닥 **32** 29
바닥이 평평한 짐배 **58** 12
바닷가재 **11** 30, **62** 13
바닷물 **91** 30
바둑판 무늬가 있는 **24** 18
바람 **80** 4
바람막이용 잠바 **19** 5
바람막이 유리 **51** 45
바람부는 **25** 13
바스 **98** 10
바이얼린 **98** 7
바위 **88** 11
바퀴 **52** 4
바퀴벌레 **63** 9
바퀴달린 의자 **39** 2
바퀴덮개 **52** 10
바퀴의 살 **52** 26
박격포 **48** 28
박스석 **99** 11
(물)밖으로 **103** 7
박쥐 **66** 4
박테리아 배양용 접시 **78** 3
반경 **79** 14
반바지 **22** 2
반사물기 **52** 25
반속치마 **22** 8
반장화 **19** 21
반지 **23** 2
반쪽 닭 **11** 17
받침접시 **16** 27, **29** 21
발 **69** 29
발가락 **4** 54
빨간무우 **7** 29
빨간색 **104**
발굽 **67** 35
발굽있는 포유동물 **66**

발꿈치 **5** 50
빨대 **16** 10
발동기선 **59** 13
발등 **5** 51
발등 끝 불쑥나온 곳 **5** 52
빨래 집게 **35** 20
빨랫줄 **35** 19
발레 **99** A
발목 **5** 49
발 문지르개 **34** 12
발사대 **75** 15
발신인의 주소 성명 **46** 8
발전기 **80** 21
발전소 **80** 20
발진 **40** 1
발코니 **99** 14
발톱 **5** 56, **68** 2
발트해 **70** 22
발판 **39** 18
발판 사닥다리 **35** 1
밤 **9** 32
밧줄 **58** 25
빵 **14** 12
방광 **5** 72
빵덩어리 **12** 7
빵류 제조 판매업자 **84** 8
방목장 **81** C
방석 **28** 24
방수복 **88** 10
방아쇠 **48** 22
방울달린 작은 북 **98** 17
방울뱀 **65** 10
빵을 놓는 접시 **29** 11
방이 여러개 있는 이층식 주택 **27** B
방충망 **27** 19
방향 지시등 **51** 50
방향 지시 지레 **50** 11
배 **4** 14, **8** 18
배관공 **85** 1
배구 **92**
배구공 **92** 22
배기관 **52** 33
배달부 **49** 10
배달원 **85** 10
배밑의 선창 **58** 8
배수관 **27** 18, **34** 9
배심원 **43** 21
배심원석 **43** 20
배추 **6** 3
배출구 **36** 6
배트 **92** 5
배핀 만 **70** 16
백 **104**
백과사전 **47** 25
(일)백만 **104**
백미러 **50** 7
백백이 짠 **24** 20
백보드 **92** 19
백열전구 **35** 22

백일초 **60** 13
백조 **64** 28
백합 **60** 3
백화점 **44** 5
밴조 **98** 5
밸브 **52** 27
뱀 **65** 9
뱀장어 **65** 4
뱃머리 **58** 5
뺑끼장이 **85** 7
버드나무 **61** 31
버마재비 **63** 7
버몬트 **73** 45
버섯 **7** 30
버스 **53** 20, **54** A
버스운전수 **54** 3
버스정류장 **44** 13
버지니아 **73** 46
버터 **18** 18
버팀대 **95** 14
번호판 **50** 28
뻗힘 붕대 **40** 13a
벌 **63** 19
벌레 (지렁이 모충등) **62** 11
벌새 **64** 2
범죄와 처벌 **43**
법원 **43** B
법원 경찰관 **43** 19
법원 서기 **43** 14
법정 기록서 **43** 15
벙어리 장갑 **19** 11
베레모 **19** 22
베렌츠 해 **70** 23
베어내기와 탈곡을 동시에 할 수 있는 농기계 **81** 17
베어낸 한조각 **13** 21
베어링 해 **70** 34
베이컨 **10** 11, **18** 33
베인 상처 **40** 16
벵갈 만 **70** 32
벤찌 **36** 19
벼개 **32** 16
벼갯잇 **32** 15
벽 **28** 3
벽 가구셋트 **28** 19
벽난로 **28** 8
벽돌 **82** 12
변기 **34** 29
변기솔 **34** 31
변속지레 **50** 17
변압기 **80** 25
별 **74** 4
별자리 **74** 3
병 **12** 3, **12** 9
병따개 **30** 6
병아리 **64** 22
보내다 **96** 5
보도 **45** 25
보석류 **23** A
보석류 및 화장품 **23**

보석상 **84** 12
보석함 **32** 4
보선공 **82** 17
보안조치 **56**
보온병 **88** 14
보온 털실 양말 **19** 24
보조원 **39** 8
보퍼트 해 **70** 15
보행기 **33** 23
보행자 **44** 12
보호 안경 **94** 28
복대 **66** 3
복대가 있거나 이가 없거나 또는 날아 다니는 표유동물 **66**
복도 **76** 12
복사기 **83** 24
복숭아 **9** 37
복숭아씨 **9** 37
본루 **93** 15
볼 **4** 35
볼링 **94**
볼링 공 **94** 6
볼링표주 **94** 5
볼펜 **76** 22
봄 **26**
봉고차 **53** 26
봉오리 **60** 18
봉지 **12** 8, **15** 25
봉투 **83** 31
부동산업자 **85** 5
부두 **58** 3
부록 **104**
부리 **64** 3a
뿌리 **61** 35
뿌리개 통 **11** 24
부모 **2** 6
부삽 **26** 13
부속품 **35** 17
부엉이 **64** 6
부엌 **30**
부엌에서 요리할 때 쓰이는 동사 **31**
부조종사 **56** 16
부표 **58** 16
북 **98** 19
북극 **70** 8
북극곰 **69** 22
북대서양 **70** 11
북미 **70** 1
북미 남서부산 새 (뻐꾸기와 비슷함) **64** 32
북 연주자 **99** 27
북쪽 **71** 71
북채 **98** 19
북태평양 **70** 9
북해 **70** 21
분광기 **78** 1
분류번호 **47** 7
분류표 **47** 6
분 바르개 **23** 32
분수 **79** D
분수식의 물 마시는 곳 **87** 19

분젠 버너 **78** 20
분필 **76** 10
분필받이 **76** 9
불 **28** 9
뿔 **66** 16a, **67** 35
불가사리 **62** 7
불꽃 **29** 26, **78** 21
불도저 **82** 27
불도마뱀 **65** 14
불 붙이다 **17** 13
불에 굽다 **31** 13
붓꽃 **60** 11
붕대 **39** 24
브라자 **22** 13
브레이크등 **50** 29
브로컬리 **6** 2
브이자형 스웨터 **19** 23
블라우스 **21** 34
블루 제이 (어치의 일종) **64** 8
비가 오는 **25** 1
비누 **34** 15
비누받이 **34** 6
비둘기 **64** 1
비디오 **100** A
비디오 녹화기 **100** 4
비디오 카메라 **100** 1
비디오 테이프 **100** 3
비버 **66** 12
비비 **69** 19
비상구 **42** 4
비서 **83** 11
비스케트 **18** 29
비울라 **98** 8
비옷 **21** 38
비장화 **19** 25
비치 파라솔 **90** 21
비행 갑판 **75** 10
비행기 표 **56** 4
빈치목 **66** 2
빗 **32** 6
빗변 **79** 24
빗자루 **35** 7
빙상 스케이트 **94**
사과 **8** 2
사냥개 **69** 26
사다리 **42** 1, **82** 8
사등분 닭 **11** 18
사람 **2**
사령선 **75** 8
사막 **71**
사무실 **83**
사무실용 큰 빌딩 **44** 1
사무 종사자 **86** C
사발 공기 **13** 23
사분의 일 **79** 31
사서 **47** 23, **47** 1
사슬 **52** 18
사슬바퀴 **52** 20
사슴 **67** 26

사이드 브레이크 **50** 15
(벼개)사이에(서) **102** 4
싸우쓰 다코다 **73** 41
싸우쓰 캐롤라나 **73** 40
사월 **104**
사일로 **81** 4
사자 **68** 3
사전 **47** 24
사중문 해치백 **51** E
사진기 **100** 8
사진사 **86** 10, **86** 4
사진술 **100** B
사촌 **3** 7
사탕수수 **60** 20
사하라사막 **71** 51
사회봉 **43** 12
산 **89** 19
산맥 **71**
산꼭대기 **89** 20
살구 **9** 25
쌀쌀한 **25** 9
삼각대 **100** 9
삼각붕대 **39** 3
삼각팬티 **22** 11
삼각형 **79** 6
삼루수 **93** 4
삼분의 일 **79** 32
삼월 **104**
삼촌 **3** 3
삽 **27** 31, **82** 15
상록용 작은 배 **59** 18
쌍안경 **90** 7
상어 **65** 5
상자 **13** 12
상자용형 스프링 **32** 18
상처를 꿰맨 바는 뜸 **39** 21
상치 **6** 6
상현 **74** 23
새 **64**
새끼고양이 **68** 5
새끼를 업고 다니는 곰 **66** 1
새끼 발가락 **4** 55
새끼 사슴 **67** 27
새끼 손가락 **5** 28
새로운 **24** 13
새우 **11** 31, **62** 8
색깔 **104**
색소폰 **98** 24
색안경 **90** 14
샌드위치 **16** 16
샌드페이퍼 **37** 27
샌들 **20** 19
샐러드용 드레싱 **18** 12
샐러드용 접시 **29** 25
생선 **11** 26
생선포 **11** 28
생쥐 **66** 9
샤워머리 **34** 4
샤워모자 **34** 3

샤워장 커튼 **34** 5
샹들리에 **29** 3
서까래 **82** 1
서랍 **47** 5
서류가방 **21** 37
서류 끼우개 **83** 22
서류 보관함 **83** 21
서류 정리원 **83** 23
서브 라인 **95** 3
서브를 넣는 코트 **95** 1
서브하다 **96** 2
서점 **45** 18
서쪽 **71** 74
석쇠 **29** 22, **88** 12
석탄 **80** 7
섞음용 그릇 **30** 24
섞인 야채 **18** 16
선 **79** A
선미 **58** 11
선반 **14** 6
선수 대기소 **93** 13
선외 발동기 **59** 12
선인장 **61** 40
설탕 **16** 13
설탕그릇 **29** 23
설흔(삼십) **104**
세계지도 **70**, **71**
세면대 **34** 19
세발 자전거 **52** 6
세발제 **34** 8
세제 **35** 25
세척제 **35** 9
세탁기 **35** 30
세탁물 **35** 28
세탁용 바구니 **35** 29
센터 **93** 27
셀러리 **6** 10
셋 (삼) **104**
셋 갖춤 양복 **21** 40
소고기 졸임 **18** 14
소금통 **29** 10
소나무 **61** 34
소녀 **2** 9
소년 **2** 8
쏘다 **96** 16
소맷부리 단추 **23** 12
소방수 **42** 10
소방차 **42** 3
소방 펌프 **42** 2
소불고기 **10** 3
소세지 **10** 7
소아용 닦음종이 **33** 8
소아용 로숀 **33** 6
소아용 분말 **33** 7
소인 **46** 9
소총 **48** 21
소파 **28** 25
소포 **46** 19
소풍 바구니 **88** 13

소풍용 간이식탁 **88** 15
소풍 지역 **88**
소프트볼 공 **92** 10
소행성 **74** 20
소형 비행선 **57** 5
소형 착암기 **82** 22
소형 카메라 **100** 2
소형 화물차 **49** 9
소화기 **42** 11
소화전 **42** 9
쏘니 휴대용 플레이어 **100** 30
쏘다 **97** 16
속눈썹 **5** 46
속달우편 **46** 23
속도계 **50** 10
속도제한 표시 **53** 8
속옷 및 잠옷 **22**
(구멍) 속으로 **103** 12
속치마 **22** 10
손 **4** B
손녀 **2** 11
손님 **15** 17
손님용 높은 의자 **16** 25
손님용 짐수레 **14** 19
손님이 둘러 앉는 바 **16** 24
손도끼 **36** 17
손등 **4** 22
손 물뿌리개 **27** 16
손바닥 **4** 29
손수레 **15** 19, **56** 6, **87** 4
손을 들다 **77** 1
손자 **2** 12
손잡이 **54** 8
손톱 **4** 23
손톱깎이 **23** 31
손톱솔 **34** 20
손톱 줄 **23** 24
쏜다 **31** 4
솔 **76** 18
술기 **101** 10
솔방울 **61** 34
솔잎 **61** 34
솜 덩어리 **39** 23
송금 환 **46** 18
송아지 **67** 31
송어 **65** 2
송전선 **80** 24
솥 모양의 큰북 **98** 21
쇠고기 **10** 1
쇼핑 가방 **20** 18
쇼핑 바구니 **14** 8
수 **104**
수갑 **43** 4
수갱 **80** 10
수건 걸이 **34** 25
수달 **68** 10
수닭 **64** 21
수도관 **35** 18
수동 브레이크 **52** 24

수동식 변속장치 **50** B
수류탄 **48** 29
수박 **9** 26
수병 **48** 14
수상 스키하는 사람 **59** 10
수선공 **84** 5
수선 및 관리 **85** A
수선하다 **39** 10
수성 **74** 11
수세공 **101**
수세미 **30** 11
수술 **41** 2
수신기 **100** 21
수영복 **90** 18
수영하는 사람 **91** 28
수요일 **104**
수용복 모양의 웃옷 **20** 13
수위 **85** 11
수저 **29** 8
수중마스크 **91** 35
수직선 **79** 2
수튜남비 **30** 8
수퍼마켓 **14, 15**
수평기 **82** 3
수평선 **79** 4
수평식 트레일러 **49** 18
수표 **15** 27
수풀 **61** 41
수학 **79**
수화물 **56** 8
순무뿌리 **7** 34
술 **16** 22
술집 지배인 **16** 21
숨통 **5** 60
숲 **89** 32
쉬흔(오십) **104**
쓰다 **77** 7
쓰레기차 **49** 6
쓰레기통 **35** 31, **87** 11
쓰레받기 **35** 8
스물(이십) **104**
스물하나(이십일) **104**
스위치 **37** 43
스컹크 **68** 8
스케이트 **94** 26
스케이트 구두날 **19** 15
스케이트 날 **94** 27
스케이트를 타다 **97** 9
스케이트장 **94** 25
스쿠터 **52** 29
스크린 **100** 14
스키 **94** 33, **95** 17
스키 리프트 **95** 18
스키 모자 **19** 16
스키장 **95** C
스키타는 사람 **94** 35
스키화 **95** 15
스키화 죄는 기구 **95** 16

스킷대 **94** 34
스타킹 **22** 6
스테레오 전축 **28** 20
스테레오 카세트 플레이어 **100** 25
스테이션 왜건 **50** C
스테이크 **10** 5, **18** 21
스테이크용 생선토막 **11** 29
스토브 **30** 20
스파게티 **18** 10
스포츠용 상의 **20** 2
스포츠 카 **53** 17
스폰지 **34** 7
스플릿 엔드(공격측의 끝) **93** 24
스피커 **100** 24¹, **28** 21
쏠다 **38** 7
슬라이드 **78** 31, **100** 12
슬라이드 장치기계 **100** 13
슬리퍼 **22** 18
승강기 **45** 17, **80** 9
승강단 **54** 11
승객 **54** 6, **55** 25
승도 복숭아 **8** 17
승마길 **87** 7
승무원 **56** 20, **75** 12
승용차 **53** 15
씨 **8** 2, **8** 8
시간표 **55** 20
시계 **23** 10, **76** 2
시계줄 **23** 11
시금치 **6** 8
시멘트 **82** 10
시멘트 배합기 **82** 25
시멘트 트럭 **49** 13
시소놀이 **87** 18
시에라 마드레 사막산맥 **71** 42
시월 **104**
시험관 **78** 9
식단표 **16** 7
식당방 **29**
식당에서 쓰이는 동사 **17**
식도 **5** 61
식료품 **15** 24
식물 및 나무 **60, 61**
식탁 **29** 7
식탁보 **29** 16
식탁용 은제품 **29** 22
신과일류 **8**
신문 **21** 48
신문 판매점 **45** 30
실내화분 식물 **61** 39
실로몬 **98** 31
실타래 **101** 24
실톱(곡선으로 켜는데 사용) **36** 3
실패 **101** 2
십다 **26** 4
심벌즈 **98** 18
심부름꾼 **86** 19
심장 **5** 64

심판관 **92** 1, **93** 17, **93** 22, **94** 16
십이월 **104**
십일월 **104**
십자형 회전식 문 **54** 12
씻다 **38** 16
아가미 **65** 3C
아기 **2** 5
아내 **2** 4
아들 **3** 16
아라비아 해 **70** 30
(하얀 고양이) 아래에(서) **102** 3
아리조나 **72** 3
아마존강 **71** 59
아몬드 **9** 31
아메리카 낙타 **66** 15
아버지 **3** 5
아보카도 **9** 33
아시아 **20** 5
아스파라거스 **6** 18
아이다호 **72** 12
아이라이너 **23** 33
아이새도 **23** 30
아이스크림 썬대 **18** 23
아이스크림 콘 **18** 36
아이스하키 **92**
아이스하키용 퍽 **92** 17
아이오아 **72** 15
아주머니 **3** 6
아칸사쓰 **72** 4
아코디언 **98** 28
아타카마 사막 **71** 50
아티초크 **6** 11
아파트 **45** 23
아팔라치언 산맥 **71** 41
아프리카 **70** 4
아홉(구) **104**
아흔(구십) **104**
악기 **98**
악어 **65** 8
안개 낀 **25** 12
안경 **21** 44
안경상 **84** 9
안구의 홍채 **5** 47
안내인 **99** 16
안내처 **47** 22
안데스 산맥 **71** 43
안락의자 **28** 16
(서랍)안에(서) **102** 7
안약 **41** 10
안장 **52** 16, **94** 20
안전모 **21** 28, **82** 4
안전용 유리안경 **78** 12
안전핀 **33** 11
알 **64** 13
알라바마 **72** 1
알라스카 **72** 2
알라스카 만 **70** 17
알약 **41** 7

알콜 **39** 22
알프스 산맥 **71** 44
암소 **67** 32
압설자 **40** 12a
압축용 고무 보트 **59** 20
압축용 매트래스 **91** 26
압핀 **76** 25
앞나리 **66** 3
앞 밤바 **51** 51
(화덕) 앞에(서) **102** 6
앞을 단추로 채우는 스웨터 **21** 26, 5
앞치마 **16** 6
애기 양배추 **6** 4
애완견 **69** 25
앵두 **9** 19
앵무새 **64** 16
야경봉 **43** 9
야구 **92**
야구용 글러브 **92** 12
야구장 **93** A
야구팀의 잡일을 보는 소년 **93** 18
야영 **89**
야영용 스토브 **89** 25
야영활동 **88**
야외복 **19**
야외 음악당 **87** 2
야채 **14** 9
야채류 **6, 7**
야채장수 **84** 7
약국 **45** 22
약 멸치개 **78** 26
약사 **84** 1
약상자 **34** 14
약손가락 **4** 27
약혼반지 **23** 3
얇게 썰다 **31** 10
얇은 화장지 **32** 13
양 **81** 10
양고기 **10** 13
양고깃점 **10** 15
양말 **22** 17
양복의 감 **101** 4
양복의 접은 옷깃 **20** 1
양서류 및 파충류 **65** B
양자강 **70** 69
양치기 개 **69** 28
양파 **27** 31
양탄자 **32** 28, **28** 15
어깨 **4** 5
어깨에 메는 가방 **21** 35
어린 양 **67** 24
어린이 **2** 7
어린이 야구 **92**
어린이 야구 선수 **92** 8
어린이용 변기 **33** 33
어린이용 의자 **16** 8
어머니 **3** 4
어부 **58** 2

어선 **58** 1
언덕 **88** 4
얼굴 **4** 1
얼굴 가리개 **92** 15
얼굴이나 손을 닦는 작은 수건 **34** 23
얼룩 다람쥐 **66** 6
얼룩말 **66** 18
얼음이 덮힌 **25** 16
얼음 제조대 **30** 21
얼음 주머니 **41** 4
엄니 **66** 17
엄지 **4** 24
엄지 발가락 **5** 53
엉덩이 **4** 15
(창문가)에 (서) **102** 1
에너지 **80**
(구멍)에서 멀리 **103** 5
(골프장)에서, 로부터 **103** 10
엑스선 **39** 1
엑스선 영상면 **56** 11
엔드와 가드 사이의 좌측전위 **93** 25
엔진 **51** F, **52** 32
엔진 뚜껑 **51** 47
여과기 **30** 7
여과용 종이 **78** 16
여덟(팔) **104**
여든(팔십) **104**
여름 **26**
여섯(육) **105**
여섯개들이 한벌 **13** 13
여성 아이들의 잠옷 **22** 21
여성용 드레스 **20** 22
여성용 중앙 버팀쇠 **52** 3
여우 **68** 6
여(배)우 **99** 20
여자 **2** 1
여자 목동 **81** 22
여종업원 **16** 2, **16** 32
여행가방 **56** 7
여행 안내업자 **84** 4
여행자 **56** 3
여행자 휴대품 넣는 함 **56** 21
역 **55** 18
연 **91** 22
연고 **41** 9
연기 **42** 15
연기 탐지기 **33** 15
연락선 **58** 17
연료차 **49** 3
연못 **87** 8
연분홍색 **104**
연소기 **30** 29
연월 **104**
연장걸이대 **36** 15
연장선 **36** 5
연장통 **36** 23
연장 헛간 **27** 28
연필 **76** 24

연필 깎기 **76** 20, **83** 30
연필 지우개 **76** 21
연화제 **35** 27
열 **40** 2
열(십) **47** 11, **80** 27, **104**
열기 풍선 **57** 1
열넷(십사) **104**
열다 **31** 3
열다섯(십오) **104**
열둘(십이) **104**
열람표 **47** 12
열린 **24** 15
열방지용 장 **27** 20
열셋(십삼) **104**
열아홉(십구) **104**
열여덟(십팔) **104**
열여섯(십육) **104**
열일곱(십칠) **104**
열차 **55** C
열차표 **55** 16
열하나(십일) **104**
엷은 홑이불 **32** 19
염소 **67** 28
염주 목걸이 **23** 7
영 **104**
영사기 **100** 16
영수증 **15** 20, **55** 24
영장류 **69**
영화촬영기 **100** 15
옅은 **24** 9
(텔레비전)옆에(서) **102** 11
예각 **79** 8
예니세이강 **71** 65
예비타이어 **51** 39
예순(육십) **104**
예술가 **86** 3
예인선 **58** 13
오디오 **100** D
오랑우탄 **69** 18
오레곤 **73** 37
오렌지색 **104**
오르간 **98** 29
오리 **11** 25
오바 **19** 20
오백 **104**
오버헤드 프로젝터 **76** 27
오보에 **98** 15
오븐 **30** 32
오비강 **71** 64
오스트레일리아 **70** 6
오월 **104**
오이 **7** 20
오전 **13** 28
오징어 **62** 5
오크(떡갈나무 참나무) **60** 33
오클라호마 **73** 36
오토바이 **52** 30, **53** 19
오하이오 **73** 35

오한 **40** 4
오호츠크 해 **70** 35
옥수수 **6** 12, **60** 24
옥수수 속 **6** 12
온도 **25** 6
온도계 **25** 5, **78** 22
올챙이 **65** 16
옷걸이 **32** 2
옷장 **32** 3
옷정리 장 **32** 30
옻나무 **61** 44
와싱톤 **73** 47
와이샤쓰 **21** 46
와이오밍 **73** 50
완두콩 **6** 17
완두콩 꼬투리 **6** 17
완충기 **52** 31
완충대 **33** 5
외바퀴 손수레 **27** 32, **82** 23
외투 **19** 24, **42** 13
요금 **55** 21
요금함 **54** 5
요람 **33** 26
요리사 **16** 1
요리하다 **17** 4
요통 **40** 8
욕조 **34** 11
옹기 분량 및 화폐 **13**
용달차 **49** 4
용도 및 산물 **80** C
우라늄간 **80** 15
우랄 산맥 **71** 46
우산 **20** 24
우유 **14** 5
우유제품 **14** 4
우익수 **93** 3
우주 **74**
우주복 **75** 6
우주 비행사 **75** 5
우주선 **75** A
우주 왕복선 **75** 14, **75** C
우주 정류장 **75** 1
우주 탐색기 **75** 4
우주 프로그램 **75**
우체국 **44** 9, **46** B
우체국원 **46** 14
우체부 **46** 3
우체통 **46** 1
우측 가드 **93** 28
우측선 **53** 7
우측전위 **93** 29
우편물 **46** 2
우편물 넣는 긴 구멍 **46** 13
우편물 배달 **46** C
우편물 종류 **46** C
우편 배달용 가방 **46** 4
우편 배달용 트럭 **46** 5
우편번호 **46** 12
우편엽서 **46** 17

우표 **46** 10
운동에 관한 동사 **96, 97**
운동선수 밑받침 **22** 4
운동화 **20** 11
운반인 **56** 5
운송업자 **49** 12
운전하다 **97** 15
울새 **64** 9
울타리 **81** 9
울타리 자르개 **27** 29
움직이는 장난감 **33** 2
웃옷 **21** 33
원 **79** 11
원거리 조정기 **28** 17
원기둥 **79** 26
원뿔꼴의 쇠뭉치 **82** 19
원숭이 **69** 14
원양 여객선 **58** 27
원자로 **80** 13
원자로의 노심 **80** 14
원주 **79** 17
원추체 **79** 28
원통형으로 말린 것 **12** 11
월식 **74** 6
월요일 **104**
웨스트 버지니아 **73** 48
위 **5** 66
(다리)위로 **103** 8
(언덕) 위로 **103** 11
위스컨신 **73** 49
(검은 고양이)위에(서) **102** 2
(식탁)위에(서) **102** 10
(양탄자)위에(서) **102** 5
위치에 관한 전치사 **102**
위통 **40** 7
윈드서핑하는 사람 **59** 14
윗팔 **4** 7
유격수 **93** 5
유니폼 **92** 9
유독식물 **61**
유럽 **70** 3
유리잔 **13** 20
유리창 가리개 **33** 1
유모차 **33** 14, **45** 27
유성 **74** 5
유아석 **50** 33
유월 **104**
유정 **80** 1
유정탑 **80** 2
유조선 **58** 15
유칼립투스 **61** 27
유콘강 **71** 56
유타 **73** 44
유흥 뱃놀이 **59**
육교 **53** 3
육군 **48** 15
육백이십일 **104**
육상경기 **94**
윤을 내다 **38** 3

으깬 감자 **18** 17
은하수 **74** 1
은행 **86** B
은행 간부직원 **86** 13
은행원 **86** 15
음료수 **14** 14
음악가 **99** 10
음악 댄스 및 극장 **99**
응원단장 **93** 20
의과 및 치과 치료 **39**
의복용 가방 **56** 1
의복을 설명하는데 쓰이는 말 **24**
의사 **39** 11
의상 연구가 **86** 6
의약품 **41**
의자 **29** 17
이동벨트 **56** 12
이동에 관한 전치사 **103**
이동용골 **59** 6
이동용 벨트 **15** 23
(2)이루수 **93** 7
이룩 **57** B
이마 **4** C
이발사 **84** 3
이빨 **4** 42
이분의 일 (1) **79** 30
이불 **32** 22
이삿짐 운반차 **49** 11
이십오전 **13** 30
이월 **104**
(2)이중문 세단 **51** D
인도양 **70** 13
인디아나 **72** 14
인부용 이동 크레인 **82** 18
인사조직 **48** B
인체 **4** A
인체구조 **4** 5
인형 **33** 28
인형집 **33** 25
인화된 사진 **100** 11
일곱(칠) **104**
일광욕하는 사람 **90** 19
일루수 **93** 8
일리노이 **72** 13
일본해 **70** 36
일식 **74** 10
일요일 **104**
일월 **104**
일인용 소형 요트 **59** 15
일전 **13** 27
일할때 끼는 장갑 **27** 26
일회용 기저귀 **33** 12
일회용 반창고 **39** 4
일흔(칠십) **104**
읽다 **77** 4
입 **4** 2
입구 램프 **53** 21
입방체 **79** 27
입술 **4** 43

입술연지 **23** 29
입체교차로 **53** 4
입체도형 **79** C
잉꼬 **64** 15
잎사귀 **61** 36
자 **76** 23
짜는 행위 **101** 30
자동 문서 작성기 **83** 7
자동식 변속장치 **50**
자동 전축 **16** 12
자동차 **50**
자동차 기름 **80** 33
자동차의 옆 거울 **50** 2
자동차 편승 여행자 **53** 9
자두 **9** 34
자라목 스웨터 **19** 13
(스폰지) 자루걸레 **35** 6
자르다 **31** 9
자매 **3** 10
자명종 **32** 8
자물쇠 **52** 13
자물쇠 제조장수 **85** 4
자석 **78** 27
자수 **101** 27
자작나무 **61** 32
자전거 **52** 15
자전거를 타는 사람 **90** 4
자전거 세우는 곳 **52** 14
자주색 **104**
작가 **86** 7
작업대 **36** 22
작업 바지 **21** 30
작업 발판대 **82** 7
작업용장갑 **27** 26
작업장 **36, 37**
작업화 **21** 32
작은 **2** 47
작은 북 **98** 22
작은 탁자 **28** 29
잔 **29** 20
잔가지 **61** 33
잔디 **27** 15
잔디 깎는 기계 **27** 12
잔디를 깎다 **26** 6
짧은 **24** 1
짧은 구렛나루(귀옆머리) **4** 33
짧은 소매 **20** 21
짧은 팬츠 **22** 12
잠근쇠 촉 **23** 18
잠근쇠 촉받이 **23** 19
잠망경 **48** 8
잠바 **19** 17
잠수용 고무 발갈퀴 **91** 36
잠수용 산소 탱크 **91** 37
잠수용의 고무옷 **91** 38
잠수중에 호흡하는 판 **91** 34
잠수함 **48** 7
잠입구 **45** 32
잠자리 **63** 4

잠자리를 깔다(개다) **38** 8
잡다 **96** 4
잡물통 **50** 20
잡지 **47** 16
장갑 **19** 1
장난감 곰 **33** 3
장난감 보관함 **33** 29
장난감의 집짓기 토막 **33** 32
장딴지 **4** 20
장미 **60** 18
장수말벌 **63** 20
재단사 **84** 6
재떨이 **16** 29
재봉 **101** A
재봉틀 **101** 1
재판관의 법복 **43** 11
쟁반 **16** 33
저울 **14** 7, **34** 32
저음 기타수 **99** 23
저음의 목관악기 **98** 14
저음의 큰 나팔 **98** 23
저자 **47** 8
저장통 **15** 16
적도 **71** 70
전갈 **63** 8
전기 **80** 32
전기 기술자 **85** 6
전기 방석 **41** 3
전기 송곳 **37** 43
전기 스위치 **32** 25
전기 테이프 **37** 34
전기 톱 **27** 25
전달 메모지 **83** 25
전동장치 **50** 25
전송탑 **80** 23
전신주 **80** 26
전원 스키 **94**
전원함 **37** 26
전위 양끝의 선 **93** 23
전자 계산기 **100** 34
전자 기타 **99** 26
전자 레인지 **30** 23
전자 음향 합성 장치 **99** 21
전자제품 및 사진술 **100**
전차 **55** 30
전축바늘 **100** 19
전투기 **48** 1
전투함 **48** 5
전화 **32** 26
전화기 **83** 15
전화선 **32** 26a
전화 플러그를 꽂는 구멍 **32** 26b
절골 **40** 15
절단면 **79** 15
절벽 **89** 21
절인 오이지 **18** 8
점원 **53** 12
점화장치 **50** 14
접다 **38** 1

접대하다 **17** 3
접수계원 **86** 17
접수처 **47** 2
접시 **29** 13
접시 닦기용 세제 **30** 10
접시닦기용 행주 **30** 18
접시닦는 기계 **30** 1
접시 물기 빼는 기구 **30** 2
접어 젖힌 깃 **20** 20
접의자 (1인용) **50** 16
접자 **36** 1
접질림 **40** 13
접착제 **37** 33
젓다 **31** 1
정기간행물 구역 **47** 15
정리하다 **17** 8
정맥 **5** 68
정비사 **84** 2
정사각형 **79** 9
정수 **79** 29
정원사 **85** 3
정원용 의자 **27** 24
정원용 호스 **27** 14
정점 **79** 21
정제 **41** 6
정제소 **80** 12
정지전 **54** 1
젖병 **33** 17
젖병의 고무 젖꼭지 **33** 18
젖소 **81** 11
젖은 **25** 15
제과점 **44** 6
제동기 **50** 26, **52** 17
제목 **47** 9
제복 **21** 45
제비꽃 **60** 16
제설차 **49** 5
제트 비행기 **57** 18
제트 엔진 **57** 11
제트 연료 **80** 31
젤리 **18** 31
쪼개다 **26** 11
조개류 **11** D
조개껍질 **91** 40
조끼 **19** 12, **21** 39
조깅길 **87** 9
조랑말 **67** 20
조리대 **30** 27
조명 **99** 4
조명등 **28** 28
조명등 갓 **28** 27
조부모 **2** 10
조수 **16** 3
조오지아 **72** 10
조이다 **38** 4
조제 식품점 **14** 1
조종사 **56** 15
조종실 **56** 13
조종 핸들 **52** 12

조카 **3** 13
조카딸(질녀) **3** 14
(골프장) 쪽으로 **103** 9
졸임용 고기 **10** 4
종려 **61** 26
종이 끼우개 **83** 28
종이 성냥 **16** 28
종이 수건 **35** 23
좌석 **54** 2
좌석 벨트 **50** 23
좌석에 붙은 음식 받침대 **56** 22
좌익수 **93** 1
좌측 가드 **93** 26
좌측선 **53** 5
최임 기계 **37** 36
쥠쇠 **36** 2, **78** 7
주간 고속도로 **53** 1
주걱 **27** 21
주다 **17** 9
주문하다 **17** 5
주사 **41** 8
주사기 **39** 27
주사바늘 **39** 26
주소 **46** 11
주악석 **99** 12
주의 요일 **104**
주자 **94** 31
주제 **47** 10
주차등 **51** 49
주차시간 자동 표시기 **45** 20
주차장 **45** 19
주택 **27**
준의료 활동원 **42** 7
줄 **46** 20, **81** 18, **89** 23
줄기 **61** 1
줄무늬가 있는 **24** 17
줄 보석 **23** 5
줄자 **36** 21, **101** 15
중견수 **93** 2
중심부 **79** 13
중앙 분리대 **53** 18
중앙선 **53** 6
중앙선 칸막이 **82** 24
중위 **93** 33
중이층 **99** 13
쥐 **66** 7
쥐덫 **35** 32
지갑 **20** 9
지구 **74** 8, **74** 13
지구본 **47** 19
지네 **63** 22
지느러미 **65** 3b
찌다 **31** 12
지도책 **47** 20
지면 플러그 **36** 7
지문 **43** 24
지배인 **83** 18
지붕 **27** 4
지붕널 **82** 2

지우개 **76** 11
지우다 **77** 3
지저분한 **24** 5
지중해 **70** 24
지하철 **54** B
지하철 역 **44** 16
지휘대 **99** 7
지휘봉 **99** 9
지휘자 **99** 8
지퍼 **101** 16
지폐 **13** 25
지프 **48** 9
직각 **79** 23
직경 **79** 12
직공장 **85** 13
직사각형 **79** 19
직삼각형 **79** 22
직선 **79** 1
직선 코스 **95** 19
직업 (1.//) : 미국의 주된 업종 **84**
직업 (II.//) : 미국의 주된 업종 **85**
직접 불에 대지 않고 굽다 **31** 14
진공청소기 **35** 16
진공 청소기로 청소하다 **38** 14
진열대 **78** 24
진찰대 **39** 6
진화작업 및 구조 **42**
찜통 **30** 3
집게 **78** 29
집게발 **62** 13a
집게 손가락 **4** 25
집안일과 수선하는데 쓰이는 동사 **38**
집옆의 난간 **27** 5
집오리 **64** 25
집의 안뜰 **27** 17
씻다 **77** 9
짙은 **24** 10
증인 **43** 13
증인석 **43** 18
차 **16** 15
차고 **27** 2
차다 **96** 3
차도 **27** 1
차문 자물쇠 **50** 1
차양 **32** 12
차양판 **50** 5
차운반용 대형 트럭 **49** 17
차장 **54** 7
차 커피 저장통 **30** 15
차탕관 **30** 28
차트 **39** 10
착륙장치 **57** 15
찬물 수도꼭지 **34** 18
찬장 **29** 2, **30** 22
참고 목록 구역 **47** 21
참고철 **83** 14
참나무 **61** 33
참새 **64** 10
찻잔 **13** 19

찻주전자 **29** 19
창구 **46** 15, **58** 21
창문 **27** 7
창문 눈 비 닦개 **50** 6
창문 세척제 **35** 10
창자 **5** 67
채우다 **26** 9
책꽂이 **47** 26, **83** 20
책상 **28** 14, **76** 16, **83** 13
책장 **28** 22
책 진열대 **47** 17
처마 물받이 **27** 10
척추 **5** 58
(일)천 **104**
천공기 **39** 15
천 기저귀 **33** 13
천막 **89** 24
천연가스 **80** 29
천왕성 **74** 17
천장 **28** 2
천장 선풍기 **28** 1
철골 나무로 된 운동시설 **87** 17
철사 **37** 35
철사로 짠 판 **78** 6
철쇠 제거기 **83** 29
철하는 표지 **76** 14
청과물 시장 **45** 28
청량 음료 **16** 11
청바지 **19** 6
청사진 **82** 6
청소부 **49** 7, **85** 9
청소하다 **26** 2
청중 **99** 15
청진기 **39** 9
체조 **94**
체조사 **94** 23
첼로 **98** 9
초 **29** 27
초승달 **74** 26
초식성 큰 도마뱀 **65** 13
촉수 **62** 12
촛대 **29** 28
총검 **48** 24
총열 **48** 23
총포탑 **48** 12
추운 **25** 10
축구 **92**
축구공 **92** 26
출구 램프 **53** 2
출구 표지 **53** 24
출발점 **95** 20
충전지 **51**, **54**
췌장 **5** 71
측면 **79** 10
측면 공격수 **93** 31
치과의사 **39** 17
치다 **96** 1
치료 및 구제법 **41**
치마 **21** 36

치솔 **34** 21
치약 **34** 16
치우다 **17** 6
치자나무 **60** 14
치통 **40** 9
칠면조 **11** 23, **64** 20
칠월 **104**
칠판 **76** 5
침 **63** 8a
침낭 **89** 26
침대 **32** 21
침대곁 소형 책상 **32** 27
침대 머리판 **32** 14
침대 발판 **32** 24
침대 스프링 **32** 18
침대요 **32** 17
침대 커버 **32** 23
침실 **32**
침팬지 **69** 16
카나리아 **64** 14
카누 **59** 2
카드식 목록 **47** 4
카라해 **70** 31
카리브 해 **70** 20
카세트 **100** 26
카세트 멕 **100** 22
카약(카누형 보트) **59** 17
칵테일 라운지 **16** B
칸 **54** 9
칸막이 작은 방 **83** 5
칸막이 좌석 **16** 9
캐미솔 **22** 9
캐비닛 **30** 22
캐슈 **9** 27
캐스피언 해 **70** 27
캔사스 **72** 16
캔탈로프 **9** 36
캘리포니아 **72** 5
캠프용 트레일러 **53** 16
캡술 **41** 5
캥거루 **66** 3
커튼 **28** 23, **32** 10, **99** 1
커튼 고리 **34** 2
커튼 막대 **34** 1
커피 **18** 35
커피끓이는 기구 **30** 31
커피 주전자 **29** 18
커피 탁자 **28** 26
컬럼비아 특별지구 **73** 51
컬리플라워 **6** 1
케이블 **52** 23
케이블 카 **55** 32
케찹 **16** 4
퀸네티킽 **72** 7
퀸터기 **72** 17
코 **4** 36, **57** 8, **66** 17
코끼리 **66** 17
코바늘 **101** 29
코바늘 뜨개질 **101** 28

코뿔소 **66** 16
코브라 **65** 11
코치 **93** 21
코카서스 산맥 **71** 45
코코넛 **8** 3
코트 **94** 13
코트의 끝선 **95** 4
콘테이너 **58** 7
콜로라도 **72** 6
콤팩트 디스크 **100** 27
콤팩트 디스크 플레이어 **100** 28
콤퓨터 **76** 3, **83** 16, **100** E
콤퓨터 프로그램 작성자 **86** 16
콧 구멍 **4** 37
콧수염 **4** 40
콩가드럼 **98** 20
콩고강 **71** 62
콩팥 **5** 70
쿼터백 **93** 32
크기 **79** E
크림 그릇 **29** 24
크로커스 **60** 9
콘 **24** 8
큰 사슴 **67** 35
큰 종이철 **83** 26
클라리넷 **98** 16
클립귀 걸이 **23** 15
키 **59** 5
킥 보드 **100** 33
킥보드(잡고 타는 판자) **91** 27
타다(자전거 말등) **97** 13
타다 **17** 14
타래 송곳 **36** 9
타박상 **40** 17
타악기 **98**
타원형 **79** 18
타이어 **50** 37, **52** 28
타이프 치다 **77** 10
타일 **34** 27
타자 **92** 7, **93** 14
타자기 **83** 10
타자수 **83** 6
타자수용 의자 **83** 17
타자용 안전모 **92** 6
타조 **6** 12
탁구 **94**
탁구공 **94** 19
탁라마칸 사막 **71** 53
탄광 **80** 6
탄알 **48** 26
탄피 **48** 27
탈것 및 장비 **48** B
탑승 **56**
탑승권 **56** 18
태양 **74** 7, **80** 3
태양계 **74** B
태양열 수집기 **80** 17
택시 **55** 27
택시 운전수 **55** 26

택시 타는 곳 **55** 28
탱크 **48** 10
터미날 **58** 29
터미날(전기선의 끝 연결부분) **51** 55
터미날 건물 **57** 16
턱 **4** 3
턱받기 **33** 20
털실 **101** 23, **101** 31
털의 결이 곱고 귀가 긴 개 **69** 24
테니스 **94**
테니스 공 **94** 1
테니스 장 **95** A
테네씨 **73** 42
테이프 **46** 22
텍사쓰 **73** 42
텔레비젼 **100** 5
텔레비젼 안테나 **27** 3
토기 **66** 13
토마토 **7** 19
토막내어 자르다 **31** 11
토성 **74** 16
토스터 **30** 16
토요일 **104**
토큰파는 곳 **54** 13
톱 **36** 8
통 **12** 6
통근자 **55** 17
통근차 **55** 14
통나무 **28** 10
통닭 **11** 16
통로 **14** 10, **56** 23
통생선 **11** 27
통신위성 **75** 2
통조림 **14** 13
(등대를)통하여(서) **103** 1
통행세 징수소 **53** 27
통행 차단물 **82** 21
투수 **93** 12
투수가 서는 마운드 **93** 11
튀기다 **31** 15, **97** 11
튀긴닭 **18** 29
튜바 **98** 27
튜브 **13** 15
툴립 **60** 1
트랙터 **81** 15
트럭 **49**, **53** 25
트럭 운전수 **49** 16
트럼펫 **98** 25
트렁크 **51** 40
트레일러 **53** 10
틀 **28** 4
티자형 샤쓰 **21** 29
팁 **55** 22
파다 **26** 3
파도 **91** 24
파도를 타다 **97** 12
파도타기용 널 **91** 25
파라나 강 **71** 60
파란색 **104**

파리 **63** 18
파울라인 **93** 9
파인애플 **8** 4
파파야 **8** 6
파출부 **85** 8
판매원 **86** 12
판사 **43** 10
판사석 **43** 16
판자 **82** 16
판자로 만든 상자 **12** 1
팔 **4** 6, **100** 20
팔걸이 **50** 3
팔꿈치 **4** 8
팔목 **4** 21
팔월 **104**
팔찌 **23** 9
팥 **6** 14
팬 벨트 **51** 53
팬지 **60** 2
팬케이크 **18** 5
팬티 **22** 3
팬티호즈 **22** 5
펌프 **13** 14, **52** 21
페달 **52** 19
페르시아만 **70** 28
페인트 **37** 31
페인트를 칠하다 **26** 1
페인트 솔 **37** 30
페인츠 사막 **71** 49
펜실바니아 **73** 38
펠리컨 **64** 24
펭귄 **64** 27
펴바르다 **17** 11
편지 **46** 7
평균대 **94** 24
평상복 **20**
포도 **8** 1
포도주 **16** 19
포도주 잔 **29** 5
포수 **92** 2, **93** 16
포수용 미트 **92** 4
포수용 얼굴 가리개 **92** 3
포유동물 **67, 69**
포장 **12** 4
포장마차 **49** 8
포크 **29** 12
포크리프트 **58** 4
포플라 **61** 30
폭 **79** 35
폭격기 **48** 2
폭탄 **48** 3
폭포 **80** 11, **89** 18
폴카점이 있는 **24** 19
표백제 **35** 26
표범 **68** 1
푸른 딸기 **8** 14
풀 **76** 17
풀과 곡류 **60**
풀 뿌리개 **35** 21

풀잔디 **27** 15
풍차 **80** 19
프라이팬 **30** 5
프로그램 **99** 17
프로판 가스 **80** 30
프로펠러 추진비행기 **57** 7
프렌치 혼 **98** 26
프리스비 **90** 13
프린터 **83** 4
프린트 물 **83** 8
플라밍고 **64** 29
플러그 **37** 43
플래스크 **78** 2
플래시 **100** 7
플레어 **51** 41
플로리다 **72** 9
피고 **43** 23
피고측 변호사 **43** 22
피리 **98** 13
피아노 **98** 1
피자 **18** 30
피콜로 **98** 12
피튜니어 **60** 7
핀 **101** 20, **23** 8
핀셋 **78** 32
필림 **100** C, **100** 10, **100** 17
필드 및 코스경기 **95**
핑킹용 가위 **101** 5
팡 **98** 11a
하나(일) **104**
하마 **66** 14
하모니카 **98** 30
하얀색 **104**
하역구 **58** 20
하이에나 **69** 30
하키용 스틱 **92** 18
하프 **98** 6
하현 **74** 25
학교에서 쓰이는 동사 **77**
학생 **76** 19
한개 **13** 18
한벌 **13** 16
한봉지 **13** 17
한장의 악보로 인쇄된 팝 뮤직 **98** 2
한조각 **13** 22
할머니 **3** 1
할아버지 **3** 2
합창단 **99** 18
핫도그 **18** 2
항공기 **57** A
항공 기관사 **56** 17
항공기 종류 **57**
항공 모함 **48** 4
항공병 **48** 20
항공여행 **56**
항공 우편 봉투 **46** 16
항구 **58**
해군 **48** 13
해마 **65** 1, **68** 11

해먹 **27** 11
해물류 **11** C
해바라기 **60** 19
해변가에서 **90, 91**
해변용 긴 의자 **90** 20
해변용 큰 공 **90** 11
해변에 까는 수건 **90** 15
해변의 널을 깐 보도 **90** 1
해병 **48** 18
해병대 **48** 17
해부 기구 **78** 33
해왕성 **74** 18
해치백 **51** 43
해파리 **62** 12
핸드백 **20** 23
핸드볼 공 **94** 12
핸드볼(송구) **94**
핸들 **50** 8, **52** 2
햄 **10** 12
햄버거 **18** 9
햇볕이 나는 **25** 4
행글라이더 **57** 6
행락용 모터 보우트 **59** 16
행상인 **87** 3
행성 **74**
향수 **23** 27
향초 **6** 9
(구멍을)향하여 **103** 4
허드슨 만 **70** 18
허리 **4** 13
허리띠 **20** 16
허벅지 **4** 18, **11** 19
허수아비 **81** 19
허파 **5** 63
헐거운 **24** 4
헐렁한 바지 **20** 10
헛간 **81** 5
헛간의 앞마당 **81** 8
헤드라이트 **51** 18
헤드폰 **83** 2, **100** 29
헬리콥터 **57** 2
헬멧 **42** 12, **52** 7
헴 **101** 12
헴침 **101** 12
혀 **4** 41
혁대 **20** 17
현 **98** 10a
현관 **27** 6
현미경 **78** 30
현악기 **98**
협의자 **43** 3
협곡 **88**
형사 **43** 2
형수 올케 **3** 8
형제 **3** 9
혜성 **74** 2
호 **79** 16
호각 **90** 5
호도 **9** 29

호랑가시나무 **61** 37
호랑이 **68** 2
호박 **7** 26
호스 **42** 8, **51** 57
호스 주둥이 **42** 17
호저 **66** 11
호주머니 **21** 41
호치키스 **83** 27
혹 **67** 33
혼합기 **30** 12
홍관조 **64** 11
홍성초 **60** 15
홍합 **11** 34, **62** 3
홍해 **70** 29
화물 **58** 10
화물선 **58** 9
화물실 **57** 12, **75** 9
화물실 문 **57** 13
화병 **28** 6
화상 **40** 18
화성 **74** 14
화와이 **72** 11
화요일 **104**
화장실 **34**
화장실용품 및 화장품류 **23** B
화장지 **34** 30

화재 **42** 5
화초 재배자 **84** 11
화폐 **13**
확대경 **78** 15
확성기 **76** 3
환 **74** 16a
환기 구멍 **50** 21
환자 **39** 20
활 **98** 7a
활동구역 **75** 11
활주로 **57** 19
황새 **64** 30
황새치 **65** 3
황소 **67** 34
황해 **70** 37
황허 강 **71** 68
회계사 **86** 18
회계원 **15** 22
회로 차단기 **35** 5
회색 **104**
회색의 큰곰 **69** 23
회전목마 **87** 5
회전익 **57** 2a
회전판 **100** 18
회중전등 **35** 3
횡단보도 **44** 4

후위 **93** 34
후진등 **50** 30
후추가루 통 **29** 9
훈련용 바퀴 **52** 1
휘발유 **80** 28
휘장 **43** 5
휘저어 섞다 **31** 8
휠캡 **50** 36
휴게소 **53** 11
휴대용 가방 **56** 2
휴대용 아이스박스 **91** 41
휴대품 보관함 **76** 6
휴지통 **34** 13
흑곰 **69** 21
흑백곰 **69** 20
흑해 **70** 26
흔들이 의자 **33** 16
흔히 요리되어 있는 음식 **18**
흙걷어 치우는 기계 **82** 26
흙손 **27** 27
흙투성이의 자전거 **52** 8
흡입용 고무컵 **35** 14
희가극 **99** B
흰개미 **63** 11
히말라야 산맥 **71** 47
히야신스 **60** 10